The

Hospitality

of

Christ

Forgiveness Bestowed and Forgiveness Received

By: JC Warfield

"I wouldn't be surprised if many marriages end in divorce largely because one or both partners are running from their own revealed weaknesses as much as they are running from something they can't tolerate in their spouse."

-Gary L. Thomas

CONTENTS

For all those who know the joy of having a broken heart.

Introduction

Do you view your life's circumstances as the framework by which Jesus Christ works in you specifically and uniquely to bring about personal righteousness (the quality of being morally right or justifiable)? God is in the business of "squaring" us all up with the gospel, one way or another, through our interpersonal relationships and trials.

If love is not flowing in our personal relationships, they grow cold by way of broken hearts, wounded egos, unresolved sin, lack of desire to reconcile, etc. A common denominator is the lack of overt acts of lovingkindness. For Christians, if their relationships fizzle with other Christians, it may be a direct result of one or both parties' abdication to uphold the gospel in truth and love, and missing mutual affection is a symptom of this failure to love or to love well.

I learned of my husband's unfaithfulness to me twenty-nine years into our marriage. By God's grace, my spouse became a faithful husband through a Christ-provoked radical change to his heart brought about through repentance. And my hope has been restored that our marriage will carry on with mutual affection and edification. Before this, how did I sustain our relationship with mostly one-sided affection? By trusting God's promise that one who suffers for righteousness' sake will be blessed. (1 Peter 3:14)

So far, my husband and I have been able to repair the ruins of our married past through gratitude. We share deep gratitude for what Christ has accomplished in our hearts because of forgiveness bestowed and forgiveness received. What does this gratitude look like? I would like to show you what it looks like in my life by sharing my story of how Christ worked within my circumstances to grow my faith and convicted my husband of his unbelief.

This is a love story, first and foremost, because the immediate and final outcome is deep and heartfelt affection for Christ and what He did on the cross to save me, my husband, and our marriage. I begin with my conversion. I have included some journal entries to corroborate or highlight certain events. They are dated and italicized and have been lightly edited for grammar, punctuation, and clarity.

Chapter 1: First Love

Bicycling along Venice Beach, California in the summer of 1990, I was twenty-one, spiritually lost but searching, hungry for lasting meaning to my life. I had moved to sunny California from Washington State in "search of myself." This was a customary thing to do from what I understood at the time, which made California the perfect stage for this scene. It was also the home of my current boyfriend and the falsely imagined love of my life. Like so many other young women who don't know the love of Christ, I expected to find true love in a man without first being right with Jesus Christ.

As I went about my exercise routine on this particular day, the view seemed to contradict itself. To my left, the awe-inspiring beauty of the ocean bore a sharp contrast to the dirty and dangerous city to my right.

I couldn't reconcile the two impressions: pristine beauty and some sort of innocent existence, juxtaposed with human suffering and some sort of guilty existence. I figured out that day that I had some serious questions about God and salvation. All that "Bible stuff" a Christian friend back home had put in my head was beginning to fester and ruin my beach-intensive search for self.

February 9, 1990 *This feeling of being lost is overwhelming, it's like I need something to hold onto and make it my "center"---and that is the quest or the reason for why I am here. Experience is knowledge.*

November 18, 1990 *A relationship with God? This question sustains its annoying presence in my mind. The ache in my heart suggests a missing relationship with something inexplicable to me now.*

May 5, 1991 *I sense my life colliding with Truth.*

Jesus said to him, "I am the way, the truth, and the life. No one comes to the Father except through me. (John 14:6)

A pivotal point to my conversion came after watching a horror movie that frightened me. The movie "Jacob's Ladder" (1990) caused me to see how easy it was to develop an evil mind, and it terrified me. The only comfort I could find was via the Bible verse that thoughts can be *taken captive through Christ*. (1 Corinthians 10:5) Although I wasn't a true disciple of Christ yet, this particular verse resonated and helped me get there.

In several ways, my search for self would lead me to becoming a Christian, but overwhelmingly, it was the weight of my accumulated and unconfessed sin that squared me up with the gospel. This wouldn't happen in California but back in my hometown.

After eight months in California, family problems brought me back to Washington. I also had a deep desire to physically remove myself from my boyfriend, who wasn't ready as I was to commit to our relationship by living together.

This wise move helped me get over my intense feelings for my boyfriend so that we broke up for good, but without Christ, I was seeking my ex's replacement. I wanted to feel loved and having a boyfriend was how I best accomplished this. Within a few months, I met an adorable guy who loved to dance as much as I did, and he became my new distraction. Because this love interest was in almost every way a perfect complement to me, when he asked me to move in with him, I did. After all, it was the customary thing to do when you claim to love someone but are not sure you want a lifetime commitment.

But Christ, through my conscience, continued to be "annoying." My personal need for salvation became clear when I no longer could stand my sin, and I sought deliverance from it.

For the wages of sin is death, but the free gift of God is eternal life in Christ Jesus our Lord. (Romans 6:23)

With my heart and mind already bending toward Christ, I finally broke, and my life spilled out as displeasing to Him. In the sacrificial death of Jesus Christ on the cross, I found the lasting meaning I'd been seeking in my life. This meant I needed to stop fornicating with my boyfriend, commit to weekly worship, and get the rest of my life right with Him.

By God's great mercy, He made me born again to a living hope–repentance and forgiveness were the unfading marks of this inexplicable and glorious transition from death to life. All of the burdens of sin sweetly disappeared due to my newfound faith, and I was in love with Jesus Christ before the summer was over. I saw the "other man" in my life through different eyes after accepting my gift of salvation. After *John* attended a church college camp, he was convicted that living with me was wrong. He, too, knew that we had to break up.

At this time, John identified as a Christian, but today he says that he didn't have real faith and therefore was faking it. I, on the other hand, thought I saw the fruit of faithfulness in his life over a period of several months while we attended the same church, hung out with the same friends, and engaged in consistent fellowship with other believers, including participating in premarital counseling with a church elder and his wife after we had got engaged. I fully believed that John was my brother in Christ and growing in the Christian faith.

I spent those first six months after my conversion establishing my relationship with Christ as the most important relationship in my life, which wouldn't have happened if John was vying for my full heart, too. After I became confident that Jesus was prominent in both our lives, I agreed to let John pursue me, at which time both our consciences granted us permission to honor the Lord by getting married.

Chapter 2: Until Death...

Just after we had been married, John started scratching his (itchy) feet for lengthy periods of time which, after visiting his doctor, we learned that eventually John would need a liver transplant due to a slow-progressing, chronic liver disease called Primary Sclerosing Cholangitis (PSC). At twenty-something, we felt invincible, and the thought that this crisis would be twenty to thirty years away allowed us to put it in the closet and go on as if life were normal.

Seven children and about twenty-five years later, our mostly good marriage had become stressful and hard due to relentless money problems and the friction built up by John's hidden infidelity. Retrospectively, his infidelity had started in about 2001, nine years into our marriage, and had been (sporadically) going on for about seventeen years. At this time, I understood my spouse to be a poor Christian in several ways, but we worshiped faithfully as a family, practiced hospitality regularly, and enjoyed many spiritual fruits together. I loved him and fully expected that he would grow out of his spiritual shortcomings.

In the Spring of 2018, John had found a job in another city. This was the breath of fresh air we needed, and the position was in a good company with good pay. But a week prior to moving, John's eyes turned yellow, indicating that his forty-nine year old liver was starting to fail. We were barely unpacked when John had to go to the hospital for internal bleeding and jaundice. The internal bleeding was surgically resolved, and he was able to hide the jaundice pretty well with his skin tone and glasses, but John was noticeably starting to waste away from disease of both heart and body. By the end of 2018, I knew that my husband had matured in his spiritual shortcomings. Hands down, his anger was his most outstanding quality to me and our kids when he was in the throes of his disease.

One thing I used to (obliviously) take pride in, especially in difficult times, was that John and I had always been faithful to one another. John would agree with me whenever I would say it to him. He says that he never thought I was gullible or stupid for being clueless to the truth, because he loved me and (obliviously) presumed God had forgiven him after he periodically, silently confessed his infidelity to Him. He has since learned that a truly repentant person seeks the Lord from a pure heart and exhibits *contrition*. The remorseful sinner is ashamed of what they've done; grieved by the pain they've caused; seeks forgiveness from those they've sinned against, and desires to be a worker approved by God. (2 Timothy 2:14-26)

Within the first two weeks of being in our new home and city, we went from normal to crisis-mode. Without a liver transplant, John was going to die. Without true repentance, which we didn't know he needed, John would continue to be spiritually dead. Looking back, it appears as if Satan had the upper hand in how John would have exited this life had he died. John was under the delusion that he was "okay." Satan helped John improperly handle the Word of Truth or John might have known that the main theme of Ephesians didn't apply to him: Salvation by grace through faith.

And you were dead in the trespasses and sins in which you once walked, following the course of this world, following the prince of the power of the air, the spirit that is now at work in the sons of disobedience–among whom we all once lived in the passions of our flesh, carrying out the desires of the body and the mind, and were by nature children of wrath, like the rest of mankind. But God being rich in mercy, because of the great love with which he loved us, even when we were dead in our trespasses, made us alive together with Christ–by grace you have been saved...(Ephesians 2:1-5)

Had it been between heaven and hell, John says in retrospect he would have gone to hell based on the following verse: *Whoever says "I know him" but does not keep keep his commandments is a liar, and the truth is not in him, but whoever keeps his word, in him truly the love of God is perfected. By this we may know that we are in him: whoever says he abides in him ought to walk in the same way in which he walked.* (1 John 2:4-6) John adds that he had embraced Christ as Savior while refusing

Him as Lord - it wasn't in his heart to forsake sinning and live a righteous life.

And "If the righteous is scarcely saved, what will become of the ungodly and the sinner?" (1 Peter 4:18)

Amazingly, John's pride and unusual tenacity prevented him from admitting he was sick, but allowed him to perform at his job for nine months while having medical procedures and random overnight hospital stays while his MELD (Model for End-Stage Liver Disease) score crept higher. Dealing with progressing ESLD (End-Stage Liver Disease) became part of our daily grind, but John did not suffer much physically in this chapter of our lives. It was the emotional toll of our relationship that was a heavy burden.

May 11, 2018 *Having to "bow down" to John's rancor is getting tedious and causing a lot of problems. He is declining before my eyes in health, yet I grieve more over his overt disregard for his bad attitude. I remind myself that God's intention is to be God, and it's up to me to cling to such power . . . John 15:5—"I am the vine, you are the branches; the one who remains in me, and I in him bears much fruit, for apart from me you can do nothing." . . . John 14:1—"Let not your hearts be troubled."*

My main issue was being alone in a new city and attending a new church with a seriously ill husband who seemed to have no desire to call out to God in his afflictions. He didn't ask Christ for anything beyond the perfunctory prayer at dinner time, and since his failing health sapped his patience even more, my pleas for mutual edification and affection went mostly unheeded. I had a choice to make, and I made the right one. I learned how to trust my Lord . . . deeply.

I waited patiently for the Lord; he inclined to me and heard my cry. He drew me up from the pit of destruction, out of the miry bog, and set my feet upon a rock, making my steps secure. (Psalm 40:1-2)

Christ would insist on his own path for my learning this, and it would be hard and messy. First, He would discipline me, and it was going to hurt a lot. An example of this is when I decided to text a friend one night after polishing off a bottle of wine. Two glasses is my limit, so another two put me in the wrong frame of mind and removed normal inhibitions.

I received exactly what was warranted for my reckless timing and sinful rantings, which was guilt and shame and the need to beg forgiveness. (Which I did, earnestly.) Despite my physical distance from my friend, forgiveness appeared to be granted. Yet the friendship fell apart as I had been blocked from being able to text her further. I was now without my closest friend, and I needed Christ even more. He provided through His Word, weekly worship, and the duties of being mom to our youngest three children.

Before the texting episode, I had reached out to a mature Christian woman from our previous church who was counseling me via email. She described my situation as God throwing me a "curveball." And what, she asked, was I going to do about it? Part of what she told me was that John and I should have better prepared for our current medical and financial situation. Her admonishments helped to stave off whining over my situation and propel me toward earning my medical coding certificate. She gave me what I needed most, which was her honest evaluation of where she thought I was spiritually lacking.

The timing of her counsel was good for another reason, being that I was being challenged, and it caused me a lot of anxiety. I knew that I had to choose between letting my anxiety rule over me or discerning the voice of Christ in her counsel. Ultimately, how open was I to hearing some truths about myself and my situation? Would I heed her voice (alone) and buckle under my vexation in an attempt to preserve myself from further emotional pain and anxiety? Or would I listen and respond to Christ in His desire to impart His wisdom to me through her?

The bad texting episode between my friend and me didn't start with me becoming drunk. About two weeks prior, I had challenged her on some spiritual issues I had become privy to in her Christian walk. Our friendship at this time consisted of timely responses involving a couple days, so after two weeks went by and I hadn't heard from her, I texted her again but ended up sinning against her with what I texted.

Five years later today, we are still unreconciled, and I'm curious if she believes she was the only one who was wronged. I'm confident that I sinned against her, but I'm inclined to believe that I wounded her more with my first text because of her definitive retaliation after the second one, which would have been dishonest on her part. All in all, this situation probably would have turned out better if neither of us was trying to repair our relationship from behind our cell phones. It was cruel and cowardly to do so. I bring this up because it is one "fizzled" relationship in my life due to failure of one or both parties to uphold the gospel in truth and love.

Faithful are the wounds of a friend; profuse are the kisses of an enemy. (Proverbs 27:6)

John and I faced several difficulties. First was the knowledge that most in his position die while waiting for a liver, since the number of donors is limited. Next, we were not united in our focus, which meant I was preparing for the real potential of widowhood alone—a horrible possibility for so many reasons. We had never planned for this day and we should have.

We didn't have a financial plan, or life insurance, so there wasn't a safety net for me and my youngest three boys should John die. In fact, we learned of John's liver disease while applying for life insurance and were denied based on his condition.

It was at this time I was dealt a sting to my loneliness in two ways. First, John received a card from a husband and wife from back home addressed only to him; it praised him for his faithfulness in this difficult time and said how much they missed him. They also praised my oldest son, but not a single word addressed me–not even a "tell JC hello." We had them over once before we moved and got to know them a little. Yet I wasn't surprised by their inflated affection. John is very charismatic and easily endears himself to others. This couple had no clue that he needed to be severely admonished and didn't deserve their praise.

Second, our fellow church-goers didn't seem to want to get to know us. We answered a lot of questions at church about John's illness, but had hospitality been extended with an intention to learn more about us personally, I would have been able to share how I was growing closer to God because of my trial, and maybe John would have been called out or challenged in some profitable way. In our time of need, I would have rejoiced in seeing Christ in the self-sacrifices of our brethren in ways other than praying for us, texting us, and inviting us to the church potlucks.

I did extend hospitality myself (John's fiftieth birthday was coming up, so I made it known to church members I was going to have them over to celebrate with us,) but I ended up having to cancel because John had another bout of internal bleeding. Because these and other events underscored Christ's fellowship with me, I trained my heart to trust the Lord that my state of loneliness was His will and therefore meant for my good.

And he who searches hearts knows what is the mind of the Spirit, because the Spirit intercedes for the saints according to the will of God. And we know that for those who love God all things work together for good, for those who are called according to his purpose. (Romans 8:27-28)

The overall reality that was unfolding was John's disobedience, as his constant neglect for all things Christ progressively overshadowed his physical decline. This fact manifested in many different ways, but John's lack of leadership in the home was perhaps the biggest consequence for which I inevitably had to compensate for it. What can I say? Then and now, the answer is the same: his spiritual flaws and failures had to be played out. The fruit of what he'd sown to that day was heavy burdens and emotional turmoil due to his disobedience as a husband and father.

Providentially, this meant a contentious home, a rebellious and hurting teenage son, an unhappy wife, and a variety of problems inherent to godlessness. But because he never behaved completely without reliance on God, and because there were times of unity and tenderness between us, this meant God's grace was with us. (1 Corinthians 7:14) John kept his sin of adultery to himself out of pride, shame, and a twisted sense of duty to protect me from the truth.

Strangely, I was joyful. This means I was dealing with unhappiness only in my marriage, not in Christ. Despite this difficult time overall, God was answering my personal prayers: He was working out my husband's pending repentance in His timing and according to His will. He was disciplining me and deepening my faith through the Word, prayer, and worship. He was strengthening, comforting, and inspiring me through my obedience.

If you abide in me, and my words abide in you, ask whatever you wish, and it will be done for you. (John 15:7)

Adding to my joy were my two youngest sons, who at the time were nine and eleven. Too innocent to internalize everything that was happening, but mature enough to sense the tension, they were a huge comfort to me. Like most young boys when it comes to their moms, they were attuned to my being happy and would do little things like hold my hand and play with my hair when I was upset. It amazes me just how vital they were to my contentment at the time and how important this was: Tending to their contentment and joy lended to my being spiritually disciplined about performing my motherly duties and concealing, best I could, the conflicts in dealing with their father. They look back on that time in their lives as when they lived in a cool new city with a lot of fun parks. I am profoundly grateful they were spared a portion of the conflict.

My teenage son was a different matter. His maturity level allowed him to fully internalize his home environment, and he was a challenge to deal with. I related to his behavior in that I saw part of his problem was his dad's spiritual neglect of him, but I couldn't comfort him, though I tried in different ways. His pain was emotional and buried and manifested in mostly wrong behavior. To this day, he is still angry and unwilling or unable to speak honestly about his feelings to anyone in our family. It's understandable to a point; when and if he submits to the Lord is within our sphere of influence, thankfully, but that's all. It's up to him to yield in his rebellion and allow God to influence his heart and decisions. We pray and expect that in time, he will come to see his own folly in blaming others for his unhappiness.

October 25, 2018 *What does God want from me? . . . Mark 12:30-31— "And you shall love the Lord your God with all your heart and with all your soul and with all your mind and with all your strength. The second is this: You shall love your neighbor as yourself."*

Via sermon notes: When life gets complicated, you must be an extremist (an all-in Christian)--its radical to live high stakes commitment. There's no consolation/compensation to loving/living for Jesus. What does it mean to love your brother? To hate him is to let him go on in sin. Love admonishes, confronts and forgives.

But I am to submit at the same time? Being that my husband is the "brother" in question? Today I took what looked to be a good opportunity to point out John's inclination to anger, and this made him angry. I'm in a cycle of futility if I can't appeal to him at some point . . . Psalm 42:5—"Why are you cast down, O my soul, and why are you in turmoil within me? Hope in God; for I shall again praise him, my salvation and my God."

Despite all the difficulties, the situation never went completely sideways. Time would eventually reveal that John's facade was being removed by the only Physician who can take His time with the scalpel as He mercifully cut out a hardened heart. We would have to wait on Him.

The Lord is not slow to fulfill his promise as some count slowness, but is patient toward you, not wishing that any should perish, but that all should reach repentance. (2 Peter 3:9)

December 11, 2018   John is being transferred to our hometown branch, but it's only a matter of weeks before he will be unable to work altogether. He said something troubling to me before church. I asked him what he is most concerned about should he die from this disease. With all sincerity he said he was worried about his legacy, how he had nothing to show for his business pursuits. When I suggested I thought he'd be most concerned about how he leaves us, he didn't walk it back.

The transition back to our hometown was easy. Despite his health, John still had strength and energy, helping load and drive the U-Haul and taking care of schooling needs, including mine, by helping me sign up for further education. It was probably the most thoughtful and wise deed of the season.

Seeing the predicament I'd be in without him, I was now an online student pursuing medical coding/billing certification, which was really cool. It felt good to be learning a new skill and it was a welcome distraction, although the program would prove to be difficult and take twice as long due to all the medical and emotional interruptions.

We were having conversations about our marriage and the plan should John die, but there wasn't a natural flow to the words. It was as if my husband was not a believer, and I began to wonder in silent fear if it were true. I found it biblically supportable that he was a Christian but lacking faith. (I was wrong but didn't know it yet.) His lack of faith didn't bode well with me, and I challenged him on this and other issues. This accomplished very little, although he did assure me that he had never cheated on me. Given his crumbling facade at this point, I was becoming curious as to what the crux was of his nastiness and anger. Needless to say, I was perplexed by his lack of affection for Christ in his time of need.

Once we got resettled in our hometown, life seemed kind of normal for a week or two. Our girls were home on college break, and the regional transplant center had us on their calendar, too. We could relax a little and address several matters of importance, such as our finances and homeschooling help for the boys, before the singular focus of keeping John alive would consume us.

Chapter 3: Good Timing

The slow grind of liver failure is like a glacier moving down the mountain—slow, steady, and inexorable. The main symptoms are edema, severe itching, fatigue, and turning yellow. There is also a slow buildup of ammonia in the brain, causing encephalopathy, which mimics the onset of dementia—frequent naps, lost trains of thought, and memory recall issues. Ultimately, this leads to coma and death.

I recall one of the loneliest nights of my married life having occurred during one of these episodes. I was engaging John in conversation about his thoughts on why it seemed God was withholding in-person fellowship from us (there were plenty of kind texts and emails), and he kept nodding off in his responses. Despite being back in our previous church with people we'd known for years, they overwhelmingly treated us with the same general apathy as those in the church we had just left. They, too, were curious about John's disease but didn't seem to want to spend time with us. After it became apparent that John was incoherent and no longer engaging with me, the serenity of the stillness of the night had a profound effect upon me: I saw my spouse, marriage, and church community as faltering in equal measure, and I was deeply disturbed by it until peace encompassed loneliness - after I capitulated to my thoughts and wept.

Those who sow in tears shall reap with shouts of joy! (Psalm 126:5)

The first trip to the regional transplant center in another city turned out to be the final one. John went for evaluation and they decided to keep him to treat his kidneys as liver failure was hurting them. It wasn't a surprise to any of us, for he looked terrible. He was swollen from edema but physically emaciated, and his green complexion could no longer be disguised. Once they started treatments, his liver failure accelerated unexpectedly. The good news was that it was just prior to Memorial Day weekend.

John and I had no idea that people "letting loose" on the first holiday weekend of the summer leads to many accidents which, providentially, can benefit others in providing donor organs. Being on a waiting list for an organ around Memorial Day weekend was, as one of John's doctors put it, "good timing." Gives the saying, "Hold my beer and watch this!" a whole new significance.

The drive to the evaluation was another testament to John's overall lack of joy and decreasing kindness—tension ruled the first half of the day. It was difficult to hold him accountable as his poor health needed to be tallied into my and the kids' expectations. But it was becoming obvious: My husband, their father, needed to submit to Christ and get over himself! Having said this, I do not deny that the Lord was actively pursuing John, in that his deep desire to do right by me and the kids was revealed regularly enough that I never felt I should just "give up" on him. Far from it, actually.

The second half of the day was filled with excitement as John's admittance into the hospital officially put him on the waiting list for a liver donor. Being incredibly sick was paying off in one way. The higher his MELD score, the higher he was on the list. John was being given the chance to fight for his life as his MELD score reached 48, the highest for a patient to have a transplant and live.

This adventure suited me in that I was trusting God and I had my own battles I wanted to win. This adventure suited John in that he refused to believe that it would end badly, or if it did, that it would be due to him not doing his part.

Today, he adds that his pride was in full force by this time. I can attest to that. The weeks leading up to the transplant were not a testament to a husband and wife deeply in love and cherishing their potential last season of life together. There were moments that were tender and sweet, but at one point I needed help in how to deal with my spouse and went to my pastor and church elders. They expressed that they, too, had concerns about John's lack of leadership in the home. For whatever reason, though, God left John and me to deal with his spiritual shortcomings alone. John did not have friends who challenged him on spiritual issues, and my pastor and elders did not step in and challenge him face to face like I thought they would. Instead, it would be me. And I trust this was God's plan all along, based on faith and on how Christ manifested Himself throughout all my personal battles that came with this trial.

May 25, 2019 *It should perhaps be a strange thing to say that life is perfectly sweet at this moment. I do my utmost to savor it, as it will pass. Considering the trial we are in, the potential of losing John, and the concerns gnawing at me, life is rich and profound all because of Jesus Himself, alive in me and through me. I'm sometimes embarrassed by my weaknesses, but I do not detest fear. It fails to grip me as I abide in Him.*

Chapter 4: The Transplant

The day that we were told a liver was approved and ready for transplant into John, joy was unleashed! From the doctors and nurses (most to whom John had endeared himself) to our family and brethren, praises were heard on high. In fact, I was texting someone about the news who just happened to be at church because it was the Lord's Day, and the timing allowed for the text to be read from the pulpit. We imagined the hoots and hollers, and the imagery was like balm: aromatic and soothing, a consolation as we awaited surgery.

If I didn't believe in God's sovereignty, I might say that I regretted that John's surgery day had not begun and ended with all things in order, spiritually, financially, and emotionally. God's sovereignty means that it's pointless to wish it had turned out any differently; His way is perfect, whereas ours is not. It shouldn't surprise you that once John was under the knife, the knowledge that he could perish did not leave me feeling numb. This great day highlighted for me all the turmoil and heartache that was my marriage, and I was a little pissed.

June 9, 2019 (Day of Transplant) *A donated liver has been assessed and approved by your doctors and on a beautiful Lord's Day to boot. You (John) were taken into surgery about noon—we don't expect to see you again until tonight, and we have been warned to expect a lot of devices attached to you while your body catches up to the trauma you will have been through, at which point you will begin the recovery portion of this chapter to our lives. "This Chapter," from my perspective, begins with how this past year has put eternal rest vividly in my mind. The stresses of the multiple hospital trips, the long list of unknowns due to this accelerating disease, poor communication from you, bad attitude as well—I wished to be spared many times! Today, a new day, not good for voicing my heart, but a very good day for you and for us, I hope. I think you are a nice guy when you're not an ass, but there's always hope that you'll be tenderhearted toward me someday.* (This was a journal entry, not a letter to John.)

A deep sense of gratitude highlighted this day as family, friends, and acquaintances sent many texts to me praising God for answered prayer. John might live another twenty years if all went according to plan.

There was deep sadness, too, on my part. I wasn't at all convinced that John was going to survive the surgery based on a surgery that had gone badly years ago, how he looked going into the operating room, and all the risks given to us by our doctors. Mostly, I couldn't shake the feeling that the good times to this medical adventure were over. The knowledge of my husband's spiritual decline was really only evident to me, and that wasn't getting fixed with his liver. I knew that if he survived, my life wasn't going to change much in one significant way unless God were to also transplant his heart in the operating room.

Twenty-two years prior to this, one of our sons was diagnosed with cancer at eight months old after pulling his hair out and crying for weeks. I could not comfort him, and it was torment feeling helpless to help my baby who was clearly in pain. The doctor's diagnosis was teething until when I was changing his diaper one morning, his legs flopped and I realized he was not able to hold them up. The tumor crushing his spine was moving toward his lungs and the neurosurgeon had to act fast, which he did, saving my son's life. I can hardly mention this experience as a mother without tears unless I speak from a biblical perspective. God spared my son, healed him, and grew my faith. I am exceedingly joyful knowing that my son has zero memory of any of it.

So when I say that the months following John's liver transplant were the worst time of my life, what I mean is exceeding joy wasn't possible—yet. Instead, God sustained my emotional aching while He continued to work out John's hardened heart. The emotional pain that came with John's disobedience was a gift to me to keep me dependent upon Christ.

He was calling on me to believe and practice Proverbs 3:5-7: *Trust in the Lord with all your heart, and do not lean on your own understanding. In all your ways acknowledge him, and he will make straight your paths.*

Be not wise in your own eyes; fear the Lord and turn away from evil. It will be healing to your flesh and refreshment to your bones.

When my angry spouse started telling me to "shut up" because he said I wasn't listening to him, I knew we had reached a new level to our spiritual warfare, which just added another chink to my armor. From my vantage point, John's self-confidence was turning into desperation. He was becoming intolerant of his sin and exasperating his family in his lame attempts to justify his bad behavior. His dismal life outside of Christ was closing in on him which might explain why he doubled down on his pride for the next year and a half.

During the first week of recovery, I told John that his surgery had taken several hours longer than the projected six hours. The lead surgeon finally showed up to tell me how it all went; he did not mince words. He told me that it was the most difficult surgery he had performed in his thirty years of practice, and that there was a lot of bleeding due to scar tissue from a previous surgery. The bleeding was so extensive that John received a steady supply of blood transfusions. I could read it in the doctor's countenance that he was fatigued, and in my opinion, he also appeared at peace. He retired two months later and I can't help but hope that he was at peace because of faith in Jesus Christ. Before he retired, we sent him and his team some local brew (we knew they appreciated beer) with a family picture and a card thanking them. It was well received.

One month after returning home from the hospital, we met with one of the surgeons we befriended through the transplant process. After we heard *Dr. Gravittz* was going to pass through our hometown and invited him to dinner at a local pub, he gave us his account of the surgery from his side of the table. He said that John died at least fifteen times, and that it was the choreography between the anesthesiologist and the nurse administering the blood that kept him alive. Not a believer, he described what sounded like a miracle to us.

Our favorite post-surgery moment happened next. Dr. Gravittz asked John if he was going to order a beer with him and me, and John looked unsure. In his heavy European accent he stated: "You have a new liver, it is for living - treat it gently like a beautiful woman." Whereupon we each raised a glass of Ale in solemn recognition of our having formed a special bond. Fashioned from a crisis in which we were able to laugh and cry together, we garishly toasted each other, John's second chance at enjoying beer, and all of life.

The other surgery that had gone badly had been in 2009. John had developed severe sepsis after a colectomy, and I was told that I needed to prepare for the worst. In hindsight, nothing was in jeopardy. John would dodge death and be restored to me. And I had my ballast in place to deal with it: corporate prayer, a friend looking out for me, and a strong faith. What stands out today is how John looked when he was being prepped for a tracheotomy in order to be put into an induced coma.

He looked more vulnerable than I'd ever seen him. Knowing this could be our last coherent moments together, his countenance conveyed regret. Little did I know that he was concealing egregious sin. John tells me that by the time of the liver transplant, ten years later, his soul was feeling the weight of his unconfessed sin and wanton pride. Christ was giving him over to his disobedience and deceit. Yet, eternal darkness was not Christ's ultimate plan. Instead, John would be granted a repentant heart, but the events that led up to it would spiritually challenge all of us.

God tests us in order to mature our faith. I felt that several of the ways that God tested me during my husband's long hospital stay were uncalled for, meaning that it was hard enough dealing with my husband's issues, yet God added to my burdens. Because I had no control over what was going to happen to my husband but had complete control over how I would react to my feelings and emotions, I believe God wanted me to feel weak so that I would call upon Him and learn that I can trust Him with everything.

Blessed is the man who remains steadfast under trial, for when he has stood the test he will receive the crown of life, which God has promised to those who love him. (James 1:12)

For example, one of the protocols for post-transplant patients is that they must live near the hospital and their team of doctors for a couple of months after being released from the hospital. Fortunately, I had my oldest son to help me when it came time to move myself in and prepare our temporary place that was five hours from home. Suddenly, because of a red tape fiasco, I had to move out. My son had already returned home, and so I had to move bins of food and clothes out onto a downtown Seattle street by myself and figure out how and where I could keep them. I was able to call upon a distant cousin of my husband's who lived in the same city, and after we got his locked keys out of his car about three hours later, I stored the bins at his place and asked him to eat as much of the food as he wanted. The silver lining: I got to spend a significant amount of time getting to know this cousin of my husband's, and it turned out to be a very profitable investment, because I got to share a lot about my faith.

Another example of the emotional hardships of this period may sound petty if I hadn't already mentioned it early, which was the imbalance of texting and interpersonal interaction. At one point, I was expecting a phone call from a close friend and greatly looking forward to it, but the call never happened *due* to a (texted) misunderstanding. God added to my loneliness, and in hindsight, I'm glad He did. We all get disappointed and our feelings get hurt, but this can propel us to depend on God. The silver lining: I spent a lot of my hospital stay getting to know Jesus Christ, and it turned out to be very profitable for my faith.

Our complaints, when under stress, come from personal weaknesses and are useful for God directly challenging where we are most vulnerable. When we trust Him with our weaknesses, we are entrusting details of ourselves to a great God Who desires to show us His common and uncommon grace. He knows our need to feel His comfort and love and uses our weaknesses, provided that we entrust them to Him, to invigorate courage and strengthen our resolve to depend on Him.

But he said to me, "My grace is sufficient for you, for my power is made perfect in weakness." Therefore, I will boast all the more gladly of my weaknesses, so that the power of Christ may rest upon me. (2 Corinthians 12:9)

This personal strength is a manifestation of the power of Christ at work within my heart. I can't hide my inability to save anyone, including myself, from hopelessness, difficulties of many kinds, and sin. He truly is my Personal Savior, because it is Christ who puts me in my trials in order to take me out of them in His timing and according to His holiness and knowledge of all things.

When the righteous cry for help, the Lord hears and delivers them out of all their troubles. The Lord is near to the brokenhearted and saves the crushed in spirit. Many are the afflictions of the righteous, but the Lord delivers him out of them all. (Psalm 34:17-19)

After John's surgery, it appeared that nothing could humble him for long, not even the doctor's post-surgery report. At one point during our "hospital vacation," I was so frustrated with him that I blurted out, "Are you even a Christian?" I had no idea then that the question shocked John and would cause him to question if he was, in fact, a Christian. He tells me this now, and to my surprise, he wanted to reach up and punch me when I said it. I had no idea that my minor jab would cause a major blow to him. Confrontation was necessary, the sort that finally gets to the source of all the crap—that stuff lodged behind the "closet door" or the sins accumulated in your marriage sucking the life out of it.

Where Christians live together the time must inevitably come when in some crisis one person will have to declare God's Word and will to another. It is inconceivable that the things that are of utmost importance to each individual should not be spoken by one to another. It is unchristian consciously to deprive another of the one decisive service we can render to him. If we cannot bring ourselves to utter it, we shall have to ask ourselves whether we are not still seeing our brother garbed in his human dignity which we are afraid to touch, and thus forgetting the most important thing, that he, too, no matter how old or highly placed or distinguished he may be, is still a man like us, a sinner in crying need of God's grace.

-Dietrich Bonhoeffer, Life Together[1]

---

[1] Chapter 4: Bonhoeffer, Dietrich. Life Together: The Classic Exploration of Christian Community, First Edition. New York: Harper & Row Publishers, Inc, 1954, 105.

Chapter 5: Egregious Sin

John and I returned home after seventy days devoted to his medical adventure. Due to a successful liver transplant, the "recycled" liver in his body was extending his life. There wasn't a welcome home party, but thankfully, there was one invitation to break bread with another family. A sister in Christ had reached out to me a month or so earlier and was faithful to fellowship with me when I would come home from the hospital to refresh and check in with the kids. That evening we spent with her family was interwoven with praise, thankfulness, and laughter. It was a lovely finish to a hellish year, and a lovely prelude to the difficult one ahead.

If one member suffers, all suffer together; if one member is honored, all rejoice together. (1 Corinthians 12:26)

<u>September 24, 2019</u> *Why do I feel so miffed and confused? I still cry almost every day. I feel as if I've been cheated in some way as life with John returns to "as was." I observe the same ungrateful, self absorbed, and thoughtless man as before and I hate him for it. "IT"- for not giving me Christ in our worst experience as man and wife; for being a jerk; for years of admitted faithlessness as a father. He says he's sorry, but for what? And to whom? There's nothing to it - sorry passes from his lips like an embarrassment and that's all. He says that we ARE moving on. I will not submit to this tyrannical call to submission. But how?*

<u>October 1, 2019</u> *He answers . . . Psalm 25:21—"Let integrity and uprightness preserve me, For I wait for you." and Hebrews 4:16—"Let us then with confidence draw near to the throne of grace, that we may receive mercy and find grace to help in time of need."*

<u>February 11, 2020</u> *John is still having major issues with his new liver. We were told that he will need another liver transplant down the road. Neither of us internalized this information at first. Later on we put two and two together and still can't believe it. We are so bored with this, but it seems God is not finished speaking regarding John's liver.*

We spent about two years fleshing out medical and spiritual problems, but I had grown tired of John minimizing his sin. He got pneumonia and had to be hospitalized, and I got a quiet home where I would think. Thinking of a rousing suspicion I had, I did so only because I was out of options for understanding my husband. My rationalization began with the sense that "something here doesn't jive." Our texts and calls exchanged at this time (Covid prevented any and all visitation) began to look all too familiar, in that John, once again, was complaining and so forth. And so I just skipped the nonsensical dance and claimed it outloud. "Something is off here. John, you're hiding something. It makes no sense to me that you aren't any different than you were a year ago, two years ago! I know I've asked this before and I'm reluctant to ask it again, but have you ever cheated on me?"

His pause and response (a sloppy half denial and admission) was all the corroboration I needed. That was good enough of an answer over the phone so I hung up. I needed to process this new information in light of how I wasn't quite broken up over my answer. In fact, after relating the news to my two oldest sons (who weren't quite as shocked as I was), I studied my medical coding for one hour.

December 16, 2020 *(day of confirmation of infidelity over the phone)* *The tears don't fall easily tonight. Instead there is a sense of relief. The pretense is up. So many years of pining after resolution to the constant misgivings of my heart directed at my husband and father to our children. Regularly curious as to the nature of his Christian faith, for my understanding in so many instances has been that "this" did not appear Christlike and required accountability, rather than continuing to witness a fellow Christian sin and not care, over and over again. I am affirmed in my belief that I do not have my husband's heart because the Lord does not have his.*

John's answer revealing that he had committed adultery shocked me. However, I wasn't surprised, in that my misery as his wife was finally making sense. But I never actually believed it could be true. As far as I could tell there was no evidence of adultery, so when John confirmed my light suspicion to the positive, it took a good hour before the cruelty of my situation hit me. It hit hard, but I must say that it was less like being hit by a train and more like I was blocking the train. Either way, I was crushed.

Although awful, hearing the truth was fruitful. I was encouraged in my knowledge that my husband had an egregious sin blocking true happiness in our marriage causing all this headache. I wasn't ready to admit it out loud, but I was hopeful. I felt that if he is sorry—truly repentant (for once), our marriage could be Christ-centered. In order to know if my hope was not in vain, I needed to face my unfaithful spouse.

But first I brought the situation to the attention of the church elders. I was operating under the expectation that John was going to attempt to downplay this, too, once he got home from the hospital. There was no way he was going to rob me of my victory. His sin exposed, I was anxious to know if redemption was involved. I thought he was just a poor Christian, not an adulterer. I needed the elders ready to back me up in holding him square with the gospel.

Chapter 6: In Sickness...

As much as I think I might have wanted to leave John as soon as I knew the truth (as is the customary thing to do), I simply didn't have the luxury. His poor health was made worse by pneumonia and he needed my physical help. There was no running off to lick my wounds and massage the stench of adultery out of my soul. Instead, the oxygen tank had to be set up by our bed, and I had to fetch things and fix meals. Literally, "in sickness and in health" had me chained to this horrible man. However, I didn't expect that the first day of being the care-giver to my just-revealed adulterous spouse would lead to a state of joy. It started after his confession, which he had written out and read aloud to me. First, let's have a short discussion on forgiveness.

I understand forgiveness to be a transaction that Christians are to be readily open to. If I had the means to leave John that day, should I have? Or should I have been prepared to forgive him? I know that I could have left him *and* forgiven him—but ultimately, where do I stand in my appreciation for my covenantal vows to him? What does God require of me, personally, in this (not very uncommon) situation?

In hindsight, I appreciate the providential way God kept me right where He wanted me, which was in a situation where Christ was going to deliver me from my trial. Today, I look back on that day as the day that all my prayer, pain, and sacrifice related to my husband's treatment of me was going to begin to pay off.

Delight yourself in the Lord, and he will give you the desires of your heart. Commit your way to the Lord; trust in him, and he will act. He will bring forth your righteousness as the light, and your justice as the noonday. (Psalm 37:4-6)

If we suffer for righteousness sake, we will be blessed. We are to make every effort to supplement our faith with the qualities expressed in 2 Peter 1: virtue and knowledge, self-control, steadfastness and godliness, brotherly affection and love.

For whoever lacks these qualities is so nearsighted that he is blind, having forgotten that he was cleansed from his former sins. (2 Peter 1:9)

Had I the means to leave my husband after learning of his infidelity, I probably wouldn't have because of what Christ has done for me and how this weighs in on all my decisions. Grace is why I am "here," which means there is redeeming grace for my husband. Having said that, divorce is a biblical option in the case of infidelity, so I'm not arguing for or against it. In my situation, Christ had my heart directed at reconciliation and staying put, and I defend my decision to not divorce based on that alone. If you have divorced or may be in the process of a divorce, this decision is ultimately between you and Christ, because He knows exactly what you are going through or have been through and why.

John recently had coffee with a husband who is separated from his wife but "not due to any egregious sin on either side." John was miffed by his lack of urgency to reconcile with her. He asked him if he thought they would have worked it out by now if they didn't have the means to live in separate homes, but their conversation was interrupted before John received a reply to his question.

In a similar situation, we know a husband who had told his wife in an email that he was leaving her for another woman. As a highly esteemed couple in our community, it was just as much of a shock to us as it was to his wife. We later learned he had admitted to a porn addiction and that he and his wife were in counseling before he divorced her.

Are there not sweat and tears involved in bearing our Christ-appropriated crosses? Christ paid the highest price for our salvation. Adultery is a hard providence for those who are called to endure its consequences for righteousness' sake, which is another way of saying it's sad and infuriating when Christians don't reconcile.

Do not withhold good from those to whom it is due, when it is in your power to do it. (Proverbs 3:27)

In the past few years, I have noticed a trend of internet-related "rifts" in my life and in the lives of others. Easy access and addiction to pornography is probably the biggest pitfall of using the internet, but just as damaging to relationships is how we use our cell phones. When we attempt to build or mend relationships through texting, we can easily obscure feelings and facts causing discord and disconnect. Online data supports that social media is a factor in many divorces. We can easily infer that a lot of people are having internet-related "falling-outs" in this digital age.

It's a shared assumption that we are very busy and use the internet for expediting much of our communication needs. This modern convenience has made it extremely common to *take the form of a servant* (Philippians 2:4-8) from behind a laptop or cell phone. I wonder who are the most credible witnesses for Christ when our "communication" is causing us to feel less and less challenged at the command of engaging one another on the battlefield. We may not be expressly forbidden to take our grievances with one another to our laptops or phones, but when we do, are we actually assuming the Holy Spirit approves this impersonal interaction involving our hearts?

My point is this: The truly righteous cannot meet anyone at the cross and walk away with malice in their heart. This is one reason why some of us don't reconcile. Those who want to be unduly offended can't afford the humility of laying down their pride. They pay the cheaper price of avoiding "their offender" or limiting their "fellowship" with them if they can't avoid them. All this spurning is because of an offense they esteem more in their heart than their need to die to self daily.

And he said to all "If anyone would come after me, let him deny himself and take up his cross daily and follow me." (Luke 9:23)

And whoever does not take his cross and follow me is not worthy of me. Whoever finds his life will lose it, and whoever loses his life for my sake will find it. (Matthew 10:38)

Chapter 7: Love Bears All Things

After John had returned home in his weakened state and called to tell me he needed help, I was at a friend's house trying to decide what to do. Since my son wasn't able to stay with his dad, I knew that it would be heartless of me not to care for him myself or send someone. I asked my friend who is very good at not intervening on Christ's behalf and followed her advice that it was up to me what I should do. I drove the mile home and parked out of sight so I could pray and make my decision.

I determined that whatever was going to happen between my husband and me needed to happen, plus, I was anxious to get a glimpse of my future. Where was I ultimately going to land in this trial? As far as I knew, I was not in sin and I had confidence in my Lord and still loved my husband. Ballast in place, I was ready to give forgiveness. It all depended on John. Was he repentant?

Apparently Christ had been preparing John for this specific moment, too. After having read his written confession aloud to me, he pleaded for my forgiveness from his knees, broken and afraid. I should be gratuitous if I reveal any of the sordid details of that conversation. He had broken his covenant with me and defiled our marriage and our bed. Perfect grace was the only means by which I could simultaneously look at my husband in complete disgust and long to see my brother in Christ spared of his emotional pain and restored.

December 21, 2020 . . . *1 Corinthians 13:1—"Love bears all things, believes and hopes all things." . . . 1 Peter 5:6-7—"Humble yourselves, therefore, under the mighty hand of God so that at the right time he may exalt you, casting all your anxieties on him, because he cares for you."*

Sermon notes describe "owning one another's sin" as part of marriage. We own the "tragedy" of that other person, as invested in each other's souls, as ONE, in Christ...

December 23, 2020 *Thanks be to God for the Cross, where the greatest moments of my existence have occurred . . . John*

14:21—"Whoever has my commandments and keeps them, he it is who loves me. And he who loves me will be loved by my father and I will love him and manifest myself to him."

Christmas-time 2020 was one of the best times of my life. I loved the Lord for delivering me from my miserable marriage, and I had reinvigorated love for my "new" husband. When we had the kids gathered in the living room so we could tell them, I can't explain how I was able to be happy as John painfully exposed his facade to them. But during this time I wasn't mourning John's sin, I was celebrating his repentance.

Forgiveness bestowed and forgiveness received. Joy then followed. Praise God! But the sin of adultery devastates the marriage vows and its consequences can't be avoided. John couldn't avoid his conscience forever, apparently, and Christ delivered him from his prison of sin. I, then, would have to make a decision with the knowledge of John's long history of infidelity. Would the gospel play out in divorce or staying put? Sinners that we are in a fallen world, I could have chosen divorce and be understood by all. If I chose marriage, it needed to be because I believe this is what pleases Christ and that pleasing Christ is what I want to do.

Chapter 8: Providence

All at once he follows her, as an ox to the slaughter, or as a stag is caught fast until an arrow pierces its liver; as a bird rushes into a snare; he does not know that it will cost him his life. (Proverbs 7:22-23)

Chilling verse! Is John still undergoing serious issues with his liver because he committed adultery? The poetic justice of our situation is not being missed by me.

Christ promises that consequences will follow the adulterer for their reckless act. Like a dog nipping at their heel, that person must endure lasting effects of their egregious sin because of how Christ especially hates this distortion of Himself as the Head of His Bride—the Church. Adultery causes Christ's covenantal bond with His Church to be in question (to the world) and this appears to infuriate Him.

He who commits adultery lacks sense; he who does it destroys himself. Wounds and dishonor will he get, and his disgrace will not be wiped away. (Proverbs 6:32-33)

The next few months after John's confession and repentance unfolded in ways that I didn't expect. The following journal entries show that I was feeling the weight of John's betrayal. How can I stay married to a cheater?

<u>May 7, 2021</u> *I wonder if John will not escape this verdict upon his liver. It's been almost a year since we were told that liver recipients with Ischemic Cholangiopathy can do okay for a year or two before problems lead to needing another transplant. It's been two years next month since the first transplant and Dr. Gravittz shared (in private) that John is not a good candidate for a second one. He's just learning what it means to be a Christian that loves the Lord!*

<u>July 2, 2021</u> *The layers to this messy marriage may or may not get entirely peeled away. I wonder if marriage can truly survive such a long wake of marital unfaithfulness. The consequences keep budding ugly*

little heads and as we endeavor to pluck them, it feels risky but necessary, and so we do. We flesh it out and it's working, greatly due to John's disposition. He behaves as if he deserves what he's getting which yesterday was my (revisited) disgust (his infidelity) expressed in great detail and volume. I am pleased with what I see as I test him, not that I am voluntarily testing him, but I am breaking new ground in trusting him and a pile of dirt is accumulating much to my satisfaction.

September 15, 2021 *Satan once derived a lot of pleasure from my husband. I make John's "betrayal" of him all the sweeter for me by maintaining my first love (Jesus Christ) over all others. I see Satan's ploy to taunt me to repay evil with evil, thus I (must) accept that one of the consequences of my husband's infidelity is I'm going to have to periodically wrestle with bouts of doubt and disgust. From the trenches of adultery where vows are spoiled and trampled, glory seems the only way up and out . . . Ephesians 6:16—"In all circumstances take up the shield of faith, with which you can extinguish all the flaming darts of the evil one."*

Recently, I came across some saved "love letters" that were written and given to John from me years ago. Many of them were sweet and reminded me of why I chose to marry him. One letter was particularly insightful because I have no memory of having written it, and it reveals a marriage relationship outside of God's will and headed for ruin.

Note that I didn't say that the marriage was headed for ruin. Our fellowship as man and wife was inhospitable to Christ with John out of fellowship with him; feasting at the Lord's table with unconfessed adultery incurred God's wrath upon John, but because of the gift of salvation in Christ, John would eventually repent. Those who prove themselves disciples of Christ have been given this gift. This is important because it shows the extent of God's grace—that it should include spouses living a lie and concealing it for years is a fearful and awesome truth.

This is important for another reason. I assume we all have regrets in life, but some of us have wasted years cultivating our sinful desires instead of cultivating righteousness in ourselves and in those we claim to love. It's a tragic misuse of our allotted time. John, like all of us, can't truly make up for his mistakes. The most any of us can do is practice our current faith and repair relationships accordingly.

Do not lay up for yourselves treasures on earth, where moth and rust destroy and where thieves break in and steal, but lay up for yourselves treasure in heaven, where neither moth nor rust destroys and where thieves do not break in and steal. For where your treasure is, there your heart will be also. (Matthew 6:19-21)

Let me jump back to 2001 and tie in another trial where both John and I were blessed in an unexpected way. We had moved to Alabama for a job. Within a year, we were prepared to move back to Washington state since the job wasn't panning out and we missed the Northwest. God had something more in store. Similar to learning about John's unconfessed sin after his liver transplant (20 years in the future), we were going to embrace a different worship style after a serious car wreck. The connection being the relevance of all our trials or difficult chapters in our lives—they all lend to the "tapestry" of our story or God's revelation of Himself through our trials.

We were scheduled to meet John's Aunt Dixie at a restaurant, so we climbed into the van on a rainy afternoon, and for whatever reason, my seatbelt wouldn't work. On the highway, we collided with an oncoming car that had hydroplaned into us. The outcome of the car accident, physically, was John broke both ankles and shattered his femur. I had deep lacerations to one leg, partially severing my patella tendon, and took a good blow to the chest that made breathing painful, and I could no longer nurse my three-month old son. Both John and I required surgery and couldn't walk, but we were scheduled to move in less than a month. The outcome of the car accident, spiritually, was more complex and interesting.

First, we thanked God that the kids made out virtually unscathed. Physically, they suffered little more than light bruises on their shoulders, manifested as outlines of their car seat belts. Then we needed to heal and ask for help. Our local church family swooped in to help cook and clean, and John's brother flew down to drive us back after my sister flew down to take our youngest back with her. We spent three months at my sister's and brother-in-law's house, from where John and I went to physical therapy and had to bide our time until John could walk and get back to work.

How this experience led us to a different church we can't exactly say, but when we saw those bruises on our children and wondered at my seatbelt, something shifted in our worldview and kept shifting over the course of our recovery.

Back in our hometown, we didn't attend our previous evangelical church long, strongly sensing that it no longer fit us. Once we visited and became established in our new (reformed) church, this began an onslaught of positive changes that would impact us in such a way that if we were to endure another hardship, like cancer, a car accident, or anything of the like, we had a new "shape" to our faith that said there is purpose in everything, that Jesus is Lord of everything, and we are to actively build His kingdom.

Almost instantly, we were inspired to pull our oldest daughter from public school, which we did. Then we had to give her and her siblings Christ in math, reading, and writing, and thus my homeschooling career began. Blessings just rolled out from there. We were disciplining more purposefully, for instance, and worshiping corporately as a family.

Did a car wreck make us "reformed?" No, but it triggered questions about how we are to live, and we thank God for it, because it brandished a desire in us to live better and we are to this day—in spite of all the hardships, disappointments, and broken promises.

God ordains our afflictions, our crises, and our sufferings like He ordains our salvation, hope, and joy.

The heart of man plans his way, but the Lord establishes his steps. (Proverbs 16:9)

Chapter 9: Grit

When John and I were in the process of waiting for a liver, I missed an obvious clue to his infidelity. Graciously, Christ prevented me from internalizing it at the time. This being His prerogative, as Lord, spared John a punch to the face that probably would have ended his life in his fragile condition. I lived in the light while my husband was being given over to the darkness. He tells me today that at one point, he wanted eternal darkness. While he was seeking to escape his burdened conscience, he wore a facade that he was a faithful Christian.

From my vantage point and every other Christian in our lives (I assume), his facade was convincing. John says it was because of his pride and how this enabled him to deceive himself and others with little shame. This shocked me at first, but then I realized that everyone behaves this way when they willfully sin. Follow the glory and you'll find the idol.

In John's case, he was consistently serving his own interests, manifested in his dereliction of duties as husband and father, but because he talked the talk and successfully either avoided or manipulated confrontation that would challenge him on how he walked the walk, he got away with his facade for a long time. Had I not been deceived by John's facade, would I have been better off—happier, more content, divorced and remarried to a better guy? Maybe.

John says he wasn't a Christian until at the time of his repentance. Prior to that, while he was in the hospital, he prayed and asked God for the right time to tell me of his unfaithfulness. He regards the many weeks of his recovery as when God revealed the truth about his unbelief, which naturally set the stage for him wanting to ensure that he had salvation in Christ.

I rest in the knowledge that the Lord has his heart and that the extent of the emotional turmoil I've endured over the years probably had more to do with my being married to a non-believer than to a bad Christian. I don't think this changes my story much, but it does shed light on why

John was so curiously awful at times, but then again, I wasn't always kind and loving either.

I believe God protected me from the full knowledge of my husband's wayward heart, or how else could He have used me so instrumentally in John's salvation and have used his disobedience so instrumentally in my sanctification? There's no need for regret or putting on a facade with joy in one's heart for laying down a portion of their life for another and seeing it pay off.

But now that you have been set free from sin and have become slaves of God, the fruit you get leads to sanctification and its end, eternal life. (Romans 6:22)

If the tables were turned, and I was the one who had lied and cheated behind John's back as a professing Christian, would I have wanted him to pursue me for righteousness? Yes, I would, because grace is irresistible to those called to eternal righteousness. I was familiar with the fullness of God's grace at the point of my conversion. It took John a couple more decades because this was God's will.

What if God, desiring to show his wrath and to make known his power, has endured with much patience vessels of wrath prepared for destruction, in order to make known the riches of his glory for vessels of mercy, which he has prepared beforehand for glory. (Romans 9:22-23)

By laying down at the foot of the cross certain rights and wants, like my right to happiness and my desire for a more affectionate husband, I synchronously bear my Christ-appointed cross *if* I walk away from the cross believing I will endure my circumstances in Christ's strength and to His glory. This is how I prove my discipleship and provide self-evidence to the power of Christ at work in me for a greater purpose than if I were to lead my own life. I believe pursuing my husband for the Lord ought to be one of my greatest passions and goals, or what kind of disciple am I? Having said that, I can only lead the life God has assigned to me.

Wife, how do you know whether you will save your husband? Husband, how do you know whether you will save your wife? Only let each person lead the life that the Lord has assigned to him, and to which God has called him. (1 Corinthians 7:16-17)

Christ ordained a repentant heart when John's physical death was (twice) at hand. This divine act conjures awe and inspiration for greater things, like a renewed marriage and transformed lives, and not just for me and John but for all those we share our story with. Jesus Christ glorifies Himself by turning misery into joy. We reciprocate His perfect hospitality with telling others about what we personally know about the loveliness of Christ.

Oh, magnify the Lord with me, and let us exalt his name together! (Psalm 34:3)

None of us is without sin or in need of redeeming grace. How and when Christ summons us to faith or deeper faith via our own circumstances is solely up to Him. We can only covet His blessings in return for our obedience.

For example, there are moments when I want to rehash the ugly parts of my marriage and feel entitled to do so. As a sinner, I don't expect this temptation to go away. Graciously, John doesn't either. We've learned to show some grit when it comes to sharing the burden of his adulterous past, of which I am owning too, inasmuch as I aim to please Christ as my first priority. This "tragedy" is part of who we are as faithful husband and wife.

On one particular day, I was having a hard time with the knowledge of John's adulterous acts, my imagination getting the best of me. This is an unpleasant consequence, but I recognized Satan at the helm of this seduction. By tempting me to form some kind of vendetta against John, I knew that if I gave in, it would be due to my vanity and that vanity would beget unnecessary marital conflict. Showing hospitality to sin was not an option.

As my imagination was getting the best of me, did I take my *thoughts captive and to the obedience of Christ*? I did, how? Offensively, of course! I put on something sexy and made love to my husband—maybe to spite Satan more than to please John. This is warfare and only a fool lets the enemy get an easy foothold. At this point, I'd be repaying evil with evil if I start "hating" my husband. My forgiveness and desire to stay married come from the overflow of my Christian heart. If, at any time, I choose to dismiss what Christ has already done in me and through me, it means I resent the sacrifices I have made for my husband's spiritual benefit. In good conscience, this simply can't be done to any personal satisfaction.

At one point in the thick of our marital conflict, I acknowledged that drinking too much alcohol was becoming an issue for me. A few things kept me from giving into this vice and becoming a drunk. Mainly, it was God's faithfulness to discipline me. He used some of my relationships to mirror the folly of my alternative for not depending on Him. He used specific individuals as instruments for self reproof and accountability that I wanted to change (such as the person I sinned against with the text). The Holy Spirit replaced shame with peace through confession (including confessing and seeking forgiveness with those I sinned against). The repentance and forgiveness bestowed by Christ brought healing and the capacity to trust Him at a deeper level.

Therefore, preparing your minds for action, and being sober-minded, set your hope fully on the grace that will be brought to you at the revelation of Jesus Christ. As obedient children, do not be conformed to the passions of your former ignorance...(1 Peter 1:13-14)

I know the peace that comes with obedience and want to keep it. Therefore, I read my Bible, confess my sin, and trust Christ to meet all my needs. Also, God graciously doesn't permit my stomach to tolerate more than a couple drinks without adverse reaction, increasing my confidence in my choice to not misuse alcohol. Lastly, Christ has proven His goodness to me many times and I've grown used to wanting to please Him. I know my folly and do not want to repeat it. The cost is too high in that Christ's gifts of peace, joy, and endurance for the next trial are mocked at the point of intoxication and are replaced by His judgment and discipline; His judgment and discipline are painful and rightfully so. I've learned to prefer to be sober and ready for a real battle. After saying this, I realize John has adopted the same biblical mindset when it comes to avoiding his sin of choice.

Due to John's need for a second liver transplant, I have lamented my desire to him to be better prepared for the upcoming medical adventure (Part II). We learned soon after the first transplant that he eventually will need another liver transplant in order to prolong his life, due to liver grafting issues that can't be surgically resolved.

My concerns involve being emotionally and financially better prepared than last time. So far, God doesn't seem to be answering my prayers according to what I see as most advantageous, and I keep having to submit my will beneath His own. I ultimately trust Him and do not value my understanding of things over His. He always comes through for me.

This means I can't badger John for my "security" or I am resisting God's perfect will, and His perfect interest in my circumstances *and* His desire to bless me. Putting my trust in Christ means I must relinquish all my expectations and allow the Holy Spirit to work in my heart. If I persist in trying to accomplish my will, I may be given over to my disobedience. Until the need for confession and repentance is met, I am living outside of God's will and suffering the consequences. (Luke 11:28)

Until repentance occurs, I might wear a "facade" that says I am waiting on God, opposite of what is actually happening. *Take me out of my disagreeable circumstances or I won't obey.* Do I truly trust Him? I can see when I truly don't in the unbiblical things I tell myself and others as a means to justify my disobedience. I know they aren't biblical because they are mostly based on my feelings and usually include lengthy "venting."

There are times when we need to *process our feelings* and look to others to help us do this, but I have learned there is a line best not crossed, which is between seeking wisdom and inviting others (because I am irked by my circumstances) to entertain the idea (with me) that Christ is insufficient for resolving whatever is causing me to cave into my emotions and complain.

Processing feelings commonly looks like two women getting very excited over how much they identify with each other's problems which is good, unless biblical solutions aren't being sought. At some point, if I'm not learning how I might step out in obedience from where I'm being challenged in my faith, it's either because this isn't my objective and I'm with a like-minded person, or it is my objective, but I'm with someone who's not walking closely with the Lord.

I have a history of not practicing my faith in all areas of life. Making excuses for personal laziness was my biggest weakness as a young believer. Today, I regret the blessings I missed out on due to my poor fellowship with the person most significant to having quality of life - Jesus Christ. I wish I'd been more diligent to read my Bible, pray, and obey when I was in my thirties.

But I have this against you, that you have abandoned the love you had at first. Remember therefore from where you have fallen; repent, and do the works you did at first. (Revelation 2:4-5)

Subsequently, I spent about half of that decade being very overweight, which (for me) was a physical manifestation of my spiritual inactivity. I was using junk food to satisfy my spiritual hunger, which didn't work, but it provided a temporary distraction from dealing with my weaknesses in the right way. Most of the extra pounds fell away by the time I turned forty and reestablished, with Christ's help, my fellowship with Him as my first priority.

In hindsight, I don't contribute a lot to how depressed I felt back then to marital distress. Although a factor, my main problem was my own thoughts. I lacked confidence and strength, and He would have supplied these things if I had only asked - *in faith.* (James 1:6) I know that I begged for these things at certain times but without actively pursuing

Christ through proper (biblical) fellowship with Him, I was merely venting and not depending upon Him. (John 15:7) Big difference!

Sanctification is occurring when I am obeying God within my circumstances. My righteousness allows the Holy Spirit to give me the strength I lack in trusting Christ to see me through my difficulty or trial. This also means that I am spiritually thriving and have an obligation to build up others.

We who are strong have an obligation to bear with the failings of the weak, and not to please ourselves. Let each of us please his neighbor for his good, to build him up. (Romans 15:1-2)

One reason I have sustaining joy in Christ and in my marriage is after John's repentance, I was euphoric for days. I previously said that I was joyful, but the truth is I was singing, dancing, and smiling for a good month. I felt God rewarding me for my obedience and warning me to not forget this time of complete happiness and why. My husband was a changed man, and in a real way we were starting a new life together. Euphoria was appropriate following my husband's repentance and being restored to me because angels were rejoicing too.

Just so, I tell you, there will be more joy in heaven over one sinner who repents than over ninety-nine righteous persons who need no repentance. (Luke 15:7)

Chapter 10: Disciples Take Risks

I have come to refer to the first two years after John's repentance as the "honeymoon period" of his repentance. In the last two years, we have had several heated arguments, all of which required us to restore our fellowship through confession and forgiveness.

<u>January 5, 2023</u> *I broke up with John yesterday. He is not living up to his promises, has said some awful things to me, and we still do not pray together. I told John that this is the equivalent of him inviting Satan to take a chunk out of my heel while he holds me down.*

Our "closet" isn't empty and this is probably the worst thing about being married to John. Working through the clutter of past mistakes, hurts, bad memories, etc. is a work in progress. I had instigated a "break-up" because John was seriously slacking in fulfilling his promises, and I knew I had to do something. We were falling back into our old way of being a couple when John was unaccustomed to edifying me. Despite all our progress, we were going to have to contend with our weaknesses as a couple.

Husbands love your wives, as Christ loved the church and gave himself up for her, that he might sanctify her, having cleansed her by the washing of water with the word, so that he might present the church to himself in splendor, without spot or wrinkle or any such thing, that she might be holy and without blemish. In the same way husbands should love their wives as their own bodies. He who loves his wife loves himself. For no one ever hated his own flesh, but nourishes it and cherishes it, just as Christ does the church, because we are members of his body. "Therefore a man shall leave his father and mother and hold fast to his wife, and the two shall become one flesh." This mystery is profound, and I am saying it refers to Christ and the church. However, let each one of you love his wife as himself, and let the wife see that she respects her husband. (Ephesians 5:25-33)

I prove to myself John is a godly man by holding him accountable to his own biblical standards of living an authentic Christian life. If we aren't truly forging ahead together, we're merely managing the ruins of our married past, and this is backsliding. As his wife and fellow disciple, I can't be a bystander in his Christian walk. I am a participant, therefore my duty is to cultivate a right relationship and loyalty for both our benefit.

Whoever pursues righteousness and kindness will find life, righteousness, and honor. (Proverbs 21:21)

"Emotional divorce" is not biblically quantifiable as a means to save a marriage from legal divorce, but in my case, emotionally disengaging from John protected me from having to compromise my reasons for excluding divorce in the first place. John promised to make up for the past, but this is undefined. I believe John either is loyal to me sexually *and spiritually* for his own sake, or he's a fool who has returned to his folly.

The backslider in heart will be filled with the fruit of his ways, and a good man will be filled with the fruit of his ways. (Proverbs 14:14)

I felt I was keeping John from recognizing where he was faltering most in his faith. He was taking me for granted, taking my forgiveness for granted, and because I held him in a sort of marital probationary period at the time, my holding him accountable to his complacency required me to *act.* I took a faith-based risk in order to call him out on his weakness.

After I had told John I was breaking up with him and why, he tried to hold my hand and I wouldn't let him. Once he accepted that I was entirely sincere in my break-up and not afraid of the consequences (such as if he became angry and retaliated and divorced me), his heart was positively impacted almost immediately.

In short, he *wanted* to become more of what I wanted which was easy for me to define: He needed to (more earnestly) pursue me and his children, which meant he had to be more intent to read his Bible and obey it. God uses the broken-hearted to win hearts, keep hearts, and grow hearts. This is what I understand discipleship to mean.

I was emotionally prepared to be broken up for a while, having peace over my decision and making my refuge in Christ. Our home lease was up in two months and so I gave John until that time to win me back. It wasn't yet fixed in my mind what it would mean if John didn't win me back, but it didn't matter because he won me back the next day.

That was two months ago and you may find it hard to believe, but John noticeably improved after I broke up with him. He says I surprised and scared him, but that it was the Holy Spirit Who drove him to want to preserve all that had become precious to him.

The morning after the break-up, I reluctantly agreed to go out for breakfast with John. He laid out some specific actions he was going to take after admitting to being lazy and falling back into some bad habits. We spent the rest of the day restoring our fellowship by praying together, speaking plainly about our issues with one another, and establishing new "rules" for us to better *Love one another with brotherly affection. Outdo one another in showing honor.* (Romans 12:10)

Chapter 11: Gaze Upon Forgiveness

I have tried a couple of times to stay mad at John, because then and only then could I claim that our main issues have not been resolved, sow seeds of bitterness, and bask in my own narrative of the past. After God convicted me of this devilish scheme, He gave me a better perspective: As much as I wish the past could be "fixed" and my wedding day "vision" realized, forgiveness is beautiful and to gaze upon it is a saving grace.

Fortunately, John's consistent walk with the Lord has enabled him to forgive me after I have swerved toward evil and said devious things in my battle of letting gratitude cover the past. As well, my consistent walk has caused me to ask John's forgiveness after I have sinned against him with my words. The mean things I have said are nothing surprising - they consist of accusing John of ruining my life and tearing him down in a variety of ways.

Keep your heart with all vigilance, for from it flow the springs of life. Put away from you crooked speech, and put devious talk far from you. Let your eyes look directly forward, and your gaze be straight before you. Ponder the path of your feet; then all your ways will be sure. Do not serve to the right or to the left; turn your foot away from evil. (Proverbs 4:23-27)

We still sin against each other, but not in big ways, because what we have achieved is spiritual compatibility, for it is active love and mutual affection that characterizes our fellowship and minimizes our fellowship friction with one another.

Finally, all of you, have unity of mind, sympathy, brotherly love, a tender heart, and a humble mind. (1 Peter 3:8)

John and I are in our fifties and have been dealing with John's health issues for a long time. Because we are fully reconciled and our marriage has been restored, we have a sense of urgency when it comes to accomplishing all that we want to before our time together is over.

Accepting our lot in life and living in the moment is what we do best together, and this disposition has afforded us the wherewithal to start several businesses over the years, move several times, and enjoy the fruits of taking "risks." We don't have any delusions as to how our plans can unravel according to His *better plan,* or to the necessity of making plans so that He can do just that. He has blessed us beyond our imaginations in several instances, putting us in perpetual wonder of just how far our faith can take us in our journey together.

To my surprise, John's last doctor appointment revealed a different picture than the one I've been mentally bracing myself for some time now. We were told that John's "numbers" show that his liver is functioning well and that this could continue for several more years. John's sideway glance and smile at me said, "See, told you so!" I am happy to admit that I took the news too literally when we were told that liver recipients with John's condition do okay for a year or two before needing another transplant. That was five years ago.

God loves to keep us in suspense and refresh us with His timing. When He removes our fixations with wrong things, He removes *dross* from our faith and aligns more of our will with His will. I rely on this action of His when I am feeling down and discouraged.

Take away the dross from the silver, and the smith has material for a vessel. (Proverbs 25:4)

Because I am emotional, passionate, and sinful, I'm essentially a created "mess" - who is going to save me? My Lord, abiding in me through the Holy Spirit, is the corralling force to my emotions and divine protector of my vulnerability. Abiding in His love keeps me from "self-preservation" - *the defensive withholding of my heart from Him and others.* Without Christ, an open heart I would not have, and its corresponding emotions of love and joy would not propel me toward obedience.

As the Father has loved me, so I have loved you. Abide in my love. If you keep my commandments, you will abide in my love, just as I have kept my Father's commandments and abide in his love. These things I have spoken to you, that my joy may be in you, and that your joy may be full. (John 15:9-11)

More than that, we rejoice in our sufferings, knowing that suffering produces endurance, and endurance produces character, and character produces hope, and hope does not put us to shame, because God's love has been poured into our hearts through the Holy Spirit who has been given to us. (Romans 5:3-5)

Chapter 12: A Weighted Comfort

May 27, 2023 *Had my love for Christ not overflowed to this human soul, then how great is my love? To attempt to reach the height and depth of Christ's love for me, I need another tragic soul by which to love sacrificially. That this soul happened to be my husband, is this not an opportunity for glory? Through Christ's great love, I was able to lay down a portion of my life for this awful sinner, whose deepest claim to my affections is that Christ enabled me to pity him like Christ pitied me in my darkest hour.*

Now that John knows the joy of obedience, our spiritual union has not been destroyed, despite the trampling of our vows by him. From here, we must continue to obey God to continue reaping the fruits that make for a good marriage. If one of us slacks, the other is not off the hook for their faith and can sustain their joy through continued obedience. Without at least one obedient spouse, strife is unavoidable.

Being mutually prideful sets the stage for destruction. We start with punishing one another by withholding affection and then follow up with more "nastiness." The right thing to do is to confess to where we know we are wrong, receive help in understanding where we are unawarely going wrong, and perceive all avenues for reconciliation in the light of lovingkindness and purposeful prayer.

Caustic acid is the devil's tool, and he wields it in our pride and spite. When my heart goes cold toward John because he is disobeying God (or vice-versa), I need to confess to lovelessness and adjust my heart's attitude toward the Cross. We have been ransomed and as servants of the same master, it's supercilious of me to demand John be a better servant. It's best if I seek to edify him as I am assigned to do (Ephesians 4:25) and if it appears as if I can't, then I must depend on our Master to discipline him according to His wisdom and power. Of course this is not easy, but God requires both of us to be sanctified in return for His sending His Son to pay the full price for our sins. (Leviticus 20:7-8)

Then his master summoned him and said to him, 'You wicked servant! I forgave you all that debt because you pleaded with me. And should not you have had mercy on your fellow servant, as I had mercy on you?' And in anger his master delivered him to the jailers, until he should pay all his debt. So also my heavenly Father will do to everyone of you, if you do not forgive your brother from your heart. (Matthew 18:32-35)

James 1:2-4 further defines what a healthy disposition looks like: *Count it all joy, my brothers, when you meet trials of various kinds, for you know that the testing of your faith produces steadfastness. And let steadfastness have its full effect, that you may be perfect and complete, lacking in nothing.*

Christians know this, but since I often hear American Christians fretting about how they might suffer when they have broken relationships and other areas in their lives that need spiritual attention, I want to remind them of their purpose to suffer in human flesh and do the will of God. The Bible speaks plainly to what being a disciple entails: *Since therefore Christ suffered in the flesh, arm yourselves with the same way of thinking, for whoever has suffered in the flesh has ceased from sin, so as to live for the rest of the time in the flesh no longer for human passions but for the will of God.* (1 Peter 4:1-2)

I'm in the habit of taking self-defeating thoughts captive to the obedience of Christ and replacing them with this mindset: Am I going to carry my appointed cross while kicking it and so forth, or will I allow it to be a weighted comfort for all that troubles me today?

Perseverance is key if we are to seek Christ and expect to find him in every situation, planned and unplanned. For me, thoughts of my husband's infidelity creep in unexpectedly sometimes, or I invite them in when I desire to feel sorry for myself. I have also learned more details about specific acts of infidelity and have connected "dots" of the past, lending to new feelings of betrayal and self-questioning. How could I have not seen what was right in front of me?

I have an answer to that. Jesus Christ is faithful to make His disciples holy by His own perfect means and according to His own perfect desires. Who am I to question how He plans my life? I believe God added the knowledge of my spouse's betrayal when it would best serve me in my relationship with Him. Am I not abundantly blessed and maturing in my faith after having learned the truth about my spouse and marriage? In my mind, it just doesn't matter how my Lord has sanctified me, just that He finishes the job. I have high hopes and aim to hear at the end of it all: *Well done, good and faithful servant.* (Matthew 25:21)

For the one who sows to his own flesh will from the flesh reap corruption, but the one who sows to the Spirit will reap eternal life. And let us not grow weary of doing good, for in due season we will reap, if we do not give up. So then, as we have opportunity, let us do good to everyone, and especially to those who are of the household of faith. (Galatians 6:9)

Chapter 13: Wait For Deliverance

My and John's last big quarrel was different in that God simultaneously convicted us individually of where we were personally disobeying Him and causing each other to stumble in our marriage. It was an intense week of revelation and acting upon what was being revealed. Also, it was purely awesome. The first notable outcome was emotional exhaustion, but second and foremost, was an earnest desire to be mutually edifying. John initiates prayer and promises to lead. I promise to respect him by following his lead. We can only account for this dramatic shift as born of the Spirit and glorifying God. *And* that we both cried out to God in our time of need and He answered.

When I think of the past and the most recent past, I find that John is a most awful sinner. Seeing myself in him has come about relying upon God in the "dark places" of my Christian walk, and John's too, and recognizing that neither of has ever lost sight of the Cross while questioning what God wants from us. *He is* the reason our marriage has traction in righteousness because there is no other earthly explanation. We have sinned horribly against one another and hurt each other deeply.

And, I am sure of this, that he who began a good work in you will bring it to completion at the day of Jesus Christ. (Philippians 1:6)

For it is you who light my lamp; the Lord my God lightens my darkness. (Psalm 18:28)

John has had to endure his share of "wounds" coming from me, while knowing his past actions have incurred a lot of them. He has consistently displayed Christ-like patience and fortitude when under fire, which speaks volumes to my belief that my husband is a changed man. I mean, where did all that insolence I had become accustomed to go?

I have changed too. Specifically, I have been stuck where I believe many women get stuck, which is falsely determining I have little joy because I can't possibly "under my circumstances" be content. If this were true, I would have to believe that Jesus Christ was the most depressed person that ever lived instead of the most emotionally-balanced and glad-of-heart. His interpersonal (human) relationships were a means to a divine end and not the mainstays of his personal happiness. That "end" is a perfect life with Him, and believers who look forward to eternal rest in Christ are probably doing so because life is hard. But, it is supposed to be. (Romans 5:3-5)

For the moment all discipline seems painful rather than pleasant, but later it yields the peaceful fruit of righteousness to those who have been trained by it. Therefore, lift your drooping hands and strengthen your weak knees, and make straight paths for your feet, so that what is lame may not be put out of joint but rather be healed. (Hebrews 12:11-13)

This profundity hit me after taking account of all the times I have witnessed others doing what I have done and with the same stagnant results, which is waiting on my spouse, friend, child, etc. to change before I will be tenderhearted towards them. I, too, have fallen into "victimhood" at different times in my life with no positive outcomes—or, in other words, disbelieving that Christ's love is all I need for having an open heart and bestowing kindnesses on those who don't elicit my immediate felt affection.

When I disobey Christ by not loving my neighbor, such as my spouse, I am "free" to hate whomever because I have gone inward and embraced deceit. (Proverbs 28:26) I won't deny there is a temporary sweetness that comes with bitterness, but it has everything to do with me and my little army of lies camping alone together in the wilderness where *The heart knows its own bitterness, and no stranger shares its joy.* (Proverbs 14:10)

In a sermon on the seventh commandment, the pastor described spouses who have grudging delight or no delight in each other as doing the bare minimum and living in "legal hatred." He reminded us that Jesus is the only safe place for our sin, and we need to bring our sin out of the shadows and into the light where there is no condemnation. (Romans 8:1-4) Otherwise, we sow and reap destruction for pursuing our own agendas instead of taking up our crosses and seeking the Kingdom. (Matthew 6:33)

Chapter 14: Miry Stretches

Recently, I was in a situation where I needed to correct a fellow believer because she was telling me that she wasn't going to feel guilty for something she had said to another woman, and I knew she had issues with guilt. It was a trivial thing and she had not sinned, and the Holy Spirit was prodding me to speak:

"All your sins are forgiven, past, present and future. You are confusing humbleness in walking closely with the Lord with embarrassment for being made to feel weak. (Knowing her well, I could be this frank.) What others *might* think of you is irrelevant to your heart's disposition. You're ruminating on past sins and present weaknesses when Christ does neither. If your conscience is clear, let your joy be complete!"

She really needed to hear that and thanked me. I was grateful, too. She mirrored my own propensity to want to justify myself to others to whom it is not owed. She got all worked up by assuming the other woman had formed a bad opinion of her when she just needed to entrust a wise decision she had made to the Lord, and let integrity preserve her. (Psalm 25:21)

This sister in Christ has a history of sexual and alcohol abuse and has attempted suicide a few times. Now in her seventies, she imputes her stubbornness to the length of time it's taken her to be happy in the Lord by trusting Him with everything. You wouldn't know it to look at her - she's pretty beat up by life and years of heavy smoking, but she has childlike faith.

Joylessness carries death, because those who bank their contentment on how others perform (love them) tend to contemplate suicide. They want relief from the pain of "bad relationships" when the Bible says, *Blessed are those who are persecuted for righteousness' sake, for theirs is the kingdom of heaven.* (Matthew 5:10) The Redeemed understand there is great depth to God's love: *Then they cried to the Lord in their trouble and he delivered them from their distress.* (Psalm 107:6) *For he satisfies the longing soul, and the hungry soul he fills with good things.* (Psalm 107:9)

I have twice entertained suicidal thoughts. The first time was shortly after I became a Christian. I had a hard time transitioning out of my "old life," especially when it came to breaking up with John. I knew that I needed to secure my loyalty to Jesus before I would ever believe I loved John in the right way, and the only way to do this was to emotionally sever myself from John *and* right some other wrongs, too. I became insecure and felt lost in those first few months of learning to walk, up until Christ sent a friend who led me to safe pasture. I assign that experience now to when I came to recognize my Shepherd's voice.

August 23, 1991 Becoming a Christian—I can't explain exactly how I finally turned to Jesus Christ, but when I did, I crumbled in body and spirit before I was made anew. Then I yearned for the comfort of my old ways but failed to convince myself they would suffice - for they can't since they never could. As I immerse myself in the Bible, I see a path before me that leads to everlasting life and a vitality swells within me that I want to travel it well!

The second time I entertained suicidal thoughts was in the aftermath of John's repentance when I fell into a pit of despair. I stopped having suicidal thoughts altogether after coming out of that particular pit. God's Word, having already been anchored to me through well-practiced faith, caused me to see the error of my thoughts within a short stint of feeling defeated and depressed.

The Lord is merciful and gracious, slow to anger and abounding in steadfast love. He will not always chide, nor will he keep his anger forever. He does not deal with us according to our sins, nor repay us according to our iniquities. For as high as the heavens are above the earth, so great is his steadfast love toward those who fear him. (Psalm 103:8-11)

Not only has Christ faithfully restored my (and John's) confidence in my decision to stay married, He's been wonderfully active in our marriage in ways that only John and I can attest to. John is responsible for having made a huge "mess" because of his past adulterous ways, which means, it is our mutual faith that allows us to navigate ourselves out of the miry stretches to our otherwise harmonious marriage. We feel bold, having become unafraid of looking like we don't have it all figured out, which is seated in a genuine desire to not "give up" when our relationship gets hard.

The more John and I rush to prayer, mutual affection grows as a direct result and as a direct insult to Satan. He can't master the quags of our sinful bents and grooves if we are seeking Christ. This might be an adventure most married Christian couples experience, but we are experiencing it for the first time. I don't think it's a stretch to say that John and I truly love each other with deep affection and lasting love. True forgiveness routinely bestowed and received has made our fellowship remarkable, and the trajectory of this is more marital happiness.

And without faith it is impossible to please God, for whoever would draw near to God must believe that he exists and that he rewards those who seek him. (Hebrews 11:6)

A large portion of John's mess is due to the fact that he was a poor spiritual leader when our older children needed him most. Being on this side of his confession and repentance, they show him affection, but it's often the kind meant to conceal deep disappointment for not having the relationship they wish they had with their father.

I appreciate this kindness our kids bestow on their dad, and my heart leaps when their countenances convey delight (or maybe it's just surprise) after John says or does something that challenges one of their bad opinions of him. I see John incrementally winning them over to Christ.

I've been asked if I regret marrying a man I had believed would be a great husband and father. Can I deny the omniscience of God? Can I say that my decision to marry John wasn't faith-based and therefore displeased God? From what I know about my Lord, He will use my children's own life circumstances for sanctifying them - if they are living out their salvation (too).

What shall we say then? Is there injustice on God's part? By no means! For he says to Moses, "I will have mercy on whom I have mercy, and I will have compassion on whom I have compassion. So then it depends not on human will or exertion, but on God, who has mercy. For the scripture says to Pharaoh, "For this very purpose I have raised you up, that I might show my power in you, and that my name might be proclaimed in all the earth. So then he has mercy on whomever he wills, and he hardens whomever he wills. (Romans 9:14-18)

Chapter 15: The Internet Factor

John asked me today if he gets a sexy centerfold in my book since it is mostly about him. That made me laugh, but it caused me to consider if I have made John out to be a villain. Honestly, if life is a race, he is my best competitor because of how instrumentally powerful he is for making me run better. Likewise, John compliments me for how I inspire him to want to be a better man. It was one of the things he thanked me for in his confession letter.

Not that I have already obtained this or am already perfect, but I press on to make it my own. But one thing I do: forgetting what lies behind and straining forward to what lies ahead, I press on toward the goal for the prize of the upward call of God in Christ Jesus. (Philippians 3:12-14)

I want to devote this chapter to the question of "formal counseling" and to discussing some of the spiritual pitfalls that come with using the internet, because they are a factor in where John and I are today. It has been implied by fellow believers that John and I are not highly esteemed. We have experienced being shunned and without any fellowship or confrontation. I find this understandable for one reason that ties into the second layer of this book: fellowship, hospitality, and the internet.

Fellowship, counsel, and hospitality are integral to leading a productive Christian life. It is my belief that these three things are not highly esteemed in our current culture and the general reason for my and John's meager experience of them during and after our trial. Bereft of these interactions with sisters and brothers in Christ, edifying counsel came at a commodity only. Meaning, when John and I really needed it, we went to our church elders.

We don't blame anyone specifically for this, because we believe most people are customarily aloof with one another as an outcome of Christian inhospitality *and* misuse of the internet. That's a topic for a different book, but I need to address it to some degree for credibility purposes.

Plus, I'm confident you already identify with how the internet negatively affects relationships.

I believe that church-goers are discouraged (or let off the hook) from cultivating fellowship and friendship with whom they don't know or don't know well, because the internet and pulpit are recognized as the main sources for being connected. This "connection" typically looks like learning about brethren's praises or burdens through emails or from church announcements. *Weeping and rejoicing* are often done through texts, posts, and emails when it's unnecessary and questionable to do so. This is one example of how I believe we use the internet as a scapegoat for not getting too close to one another.

The Holy Spirit can't engage us for edification purposes through electronic communication but perhaps minimally. A direct outcome of this stunted fellowship is how it predisposes us to flattery. We tend to complement one another in our texts. I think we are compensating for the impersonal and cold nature of constantly communicating in this way.

I appeal to you therefore, brothers, by the mercies of God, to present your bodies as a living sacrifice, holy and acceptable to God, which is your spiritual worship. (Romans 12:1)

Incessantly communicating without eye contact and body language, we remove fellowship friction and are indisposed for realizing and internalizing the sacrifices we ought to make for one another as part of our sanctification. This is spiritual monotony for those who want to practice their faith. Investing time in people has become uncommon, and if you are unaware of this for yourself, you can engage the internet for the statistics supporting the high number of well-intentioned souls who feel isolated and alone. As a culture, we have yet to call each other out on this "stumbling block," and I wonder if it doesn't have something to do with our becoming one with our cell phones.

The idols of the nations are silver and gold, the work of human hands. They have mouths, but do not speak; they have eyes, but do not see; they have ears, but do not hear, nor is there any breath in their mouths. Those who make them become like them, so do all who trust in them. (Psalm 136:15-19)

Many of us are not making eye-contact when we enter and leave our pews - why? Because we feel lovelessness around us and it's uncomfortable? Because we know we are directly and indirectly responsible for it? Direct eye contact precedes a *holy kiss* and is our first exchange in acknowledging our fellowship in Christ, but it also sets a positive tone for following through on our promise to serve one another. By not looking at each other, the message *"leave me alone as I do you"* is sent. We are leaving each other quite alone, but it is okay because we don't identify with setting a negative tone. As long as we answer the question "How are You?" - with - "Fine" or "Good" - and include a few supporting sentences, the fellowship box is checked.

Emotionally disconnected, by default of loose or non-existent fellowship, we lean heavily toward apathy when it comes to being burden-carriers. Christ's fellowship with us is up-close and personal, so He is consequently less magnified when we have little to share with one another face-to-face and from our hearts.

A new commandment I give to you, that you love one another, just as I have loved you, you also are to love one another. By this all people will know that you are my disciples, if you have love for one another. (John 14:34-35)

Those who have expressed low opinions of us, John and I know as acquaintances only since we have no history of breaking bread and sharing our life experiences with them. They don't know our hearts any more than we know theirs. The many "electronic interactions" between us could be seen as a tacit understanding that we didn't want to know one another well or they could be seen as a tacit admission of guilt for not knowing one another as well as we should. For we worshiped together for many years and had promised to love one another.

We know a couple who left our church after the husband had responded to church discipline and repented publicly to adultery. They told us that they felt vulnerable and longed for a closer church community where they could be open about their story and share their life experiences for the purpose of blessing others. Had we not heard this directly from them, we would have wondered at their departure with others who also worshiped with them for many years. The consensus is they didn't leave for negative reasons.

It is generally assumed that people in our predicament need formal counseling and I don't disagree with this - I would just argue that the "formal" part might be less assumed and needed, and across the board, if we were more active to engage one another as formal disciples.

John and I have not received formal counseling and don't see any reason to do so at this time. The Holy Spirit working directly on our consciences has been sufficient, which is not to suggest formal counseling couldn't have helped us, but He, knowing our situation, has led John and I into victory without it. Maybe because He knew we couldn't afford it at the onset of John's repentance, or perhaps He was accommodating the fact that John was sick and homebound at the time, or maybe because the Bible is full of wisdom on this issue, and if willing, an adulterer and their spouse can recover without additional resources. By *leading us into victory* I mean being in fellowship with Christ and seeing Him answer all our prayers.

The closest we have come to meeting with a licensed or trained counselor is when we were interacting with a pastor/marriage counselor while I was working on this book a year and a half after John's repentance. I asked him if he would read my (first) manuscript and give me feedback. He read it, spent time with us after accepting our invitations for hospitality, and complimented John and I on our marital progress, telling us that whatever we were doing to keep doing it.

For me, this meant I needed to keep writing my book and keep pursuing Christ. John says if we didn't cling to each other and Christ, or had I made the ultimatum of "counseling or else" - he'd have done whatever it took to keep me in his life. In our case, we both wanted reconciliation, making our situation much less complicated than if only one of us wanted it.

Really, before today's American quality of life, how did the beaten down get back on their feet? If they had Christ, they did it through their Bibles and the counsel/assistance of other believers. Not only *have* we gone through counseling, we must continue to depend upon Christ for all that we need and want. Again, this is not to say that a faithful Christian who is experienced in dealing with marital problems could not bless us. I'm simply endorsing that Christ is *indeed* sufficient because it is He who gives us every good thing.

If any of you lacks wisdom, let him ask God, who gives generously to all who ask without reproach, and it will be given him. But let him ask in faith, with no doubting, for the one who doubts is like a wave of the sea that is driven and tossed by the wind. (James 1:5-8)

Interestingly, the pastor/marriage counselor, whom we spent some quality time with, had a quick wit and penchant for telling jokes, but revealed that he was a widower (his wife passed away six years prior) and golfed a lot in order to distract himself from his loneliness. When I asked him about doing something about his loneliness, such as spending more time with other believers, he said that hospitality is experienced in many different ways. True, but if it doesn't include interactions that comfort him and remind all those present of why they have joy in Christ, then it's just *hanging out* and not fellowship. I tried suggesting this to him, but that's when he said hospitality is experienced in different ways.

I disagree when it comes to Christian hospitality. I believe he was experiencing very little Christian hospitality, and his intense relationship with golf was protecting him from feeling the full impact of how unloved he felt within his Christian community. Being a guy, he probably would deny this, but we never did get to the bottom of why he not only arbitrarily confessed his loneliness to John and me but also chose to add which vice he used for coping with it. I was irritated by his cavalier attitude at first, but now I think it's prevalent in our culture. Many Americans are coping with feelings of depression.

Do not be slothful in zeal, be fervent in spirit, serve the Lord. Rejoice in hope, be patient in tribulation, be constant in prayer. Contribute to the needs of the saints and seek to show hospitality. (Romans 12:12-13)

And let us consider how to stir up one another to love and good works, not neglecting to meet together, as is the habit of some, but encouraging one another, and all the more as you see the Day drawing near. (Hebrews 10:24-25)

Many American Christians claim to be lonely and/or have anxiety on a daily basis, which reflects hopelessness, which reflects an emotional disconnect with the message of the gospel. I believe what may constitute a heavy need for licensed counselors and therapists today is unprecedented despair caused by Christians denying one another consistent (and persistent) fellowship, and believers are helping maintain the status quo regarding our current culture's push for therapeutic and drug intervention for the depressed.

Deprivation of discipleship emphasizes a disciple's weaknesses, which leads to compunction and being depressed, lonely, fearful, etc. This begs an evaluation of our loyalty to faithfully sow seeds of maturity in other Christians. By comparison, bearing *much fruit* means we are having an impact in our sphere of spiritual influence, whereas if we are bearing little fruit, this advocates we lack zeal for Christ and are contributing to oppression.

It is the fellowship of the Cross to experience the burden of the other. If one does not experience it, the fellowship he belongs to is not Christian. If any member refuses to bear that burden, he denies the law of Christ...To bear the burden of the other person means involvement with the created reality of the other, to accept and affirm it, and, in bearing with it, to break through to the point where we take joy in it.—Dietrich Bonhoeffer, *Life Together*[2]

---

[2] Chapter 15: Bonhoeffer, Dietrich. Life Together: The Classic Exploration of Christian Community, First Edition. New York: Harper & Row Publishers, Inc, 1954, 101.

Chapter 16: Why John Cheated

John attributes his sinful pride and disbelief in Christ to his committing adultery. But he credits the hours he spent consuming his dad's playboy magazines and hardcore black and white porn images to his having an unhealthy view of sex as a young man. What made him perceptible to porn and the pitfalls therein, as an adult, began when he was five years old and left to his own devices.

His parents divorced when he was seven years old, and John was raised by his mother in another state. His father didn't pay child-support, was promiscuous, and had little contact with John. Their current relationship, although amicable, is strained by a history of unconfessed lies, most of which his father is responsible for but seemingly unable to talk about, and probably because he isn't spiritually equipped for dealing with the truth about his own failures as a man.

Although he never developed a porn habit, it was part of who John was and instrumental in sustaining and entertaining his lust for other women. In his case, it was only a matter of time before he stopped denying himself what he really wanted, which, at the crux of it, wasn't illicit sex but escape from how he felt about himself.

John says he hated himself for being a failure. He wasn't living up to his expectations in his personal life, especially in his career, and he wanted to feel good about himself. Cheating was his "drug" and something he did when he needed a *fix*. Like any good drug addict, he thought he could quit on his own and believed he had quit several times.

John began questioning if he was a Christian after I directly challenged him on this point. Once his eyes were open to the truth, which was that he needed salvation, John realized his first offense was his rebellion against God. After confessing Christ as Lord and surrendering his life to Him, he repented of all his other known sins and began living in obedience to the Bible.

Blessed are those whose lawless deeds are forgiven, and whose sins are covered; blessed is the man against whom the Lord will not count his sin. (Romans 4:7-8)

One thing I am grateful for, under the circumstances, is that John didn't have an affair with anyone I know. We haven't discussed the "other women" much for obvious reasons, but one of the incidents he did share with me involved a married woman who complained about her husband not loving her anymore. She was sad and seeking comfort in the wrong way. I felt a pang of compassion for her.

Another (cliche) incident was revealed to me immediately following John's confession because I asked for details to understand the extent of his infidelity. Was it one woman, and did he love her? *And so forth.* This incident sticks with me and I want to mention it for only one reason.

Retributive justification. This woman (in context of what I know) fits the image of the proverbial adulteress and there is a part of me that wants to find her, pick a fight, and lay her flat, but I know I would not be satisfied one iota. Scripture paints a vivid picture of enticing and dangerous harlots *and their demise.* Being in the Spirit, I hate her sin, pity her lost soul, and detest her lack of morals. If we are ever to meet, I expect I will challenge her spiritually and if the opportunity presents itself, John expects he will ask her to forgive him for how he sinned against her.

For the lips of a forbidden woman drip honey, and her speech is smoother than oil, but in the end she is bitter as wormwood, sharp as a two-edged sword. Her feet go down to death; her steps follow the path to Sheol; she does not ponder the path of life; her ways wander, and she does not know it. (Proverbs 5:3-6)

Our mutual acquiescence to put Christ first in our relationship comes with an understanding that John sinned egregiously. As a former *tare,* he was baptized and took communion, led others in prayer, and professed heartfelt faith as an adulterer. But his transgressions have been covered by the redemptive blood of Jesus Christ, through faith, so we waste our (remainder of) time if we dwell on the past. We are indebted to live for the Lord and *Owe no one anything, except to love each other, for the one who loves another has fulfilled the law.* (Romans 13:8)

Chapter 17: Covenant Presumption

I have asked myself why I sometimes am looking for a way to get out of my marriage. Having learned the underlying reason to all other "reasons," I am suspicious of my strong inclination toward stubbornness - or *natural bent* toward wanting to deviate from God. The more a Christian deviates from obedience, the more they will want to sin. Unfortunately, all sinners tend to deviate from God at times. The preemptive goal is to secure your affection for Christ by clinging to Him.

And he said to him, "You shall love the Lord your God with all your heart and with all your soul and with all your mind." (Matthew 22:37)

How does a bone-weary wife change her situation without opting for a change, such as divorce? The key is to lean hard on God for moment-to-moment grace.

I dwell with him who is of contrite and lowly spirit, to revive the spirit of the lowly, and to revive the heart of the contrite. (Isaiah 57:15)

If you are joyless, resentful, bored, or seething with discontentment, God is withholding grace either because you aren't a Christian or you are abusing your privileges. (Ephesian 1:3-14) The most obvious "abuse" being that you are not using your freedom in Christ to glorify Him in your marriage. We who enjoy many comforts in this life can easily forget it is our duty to maintain and pursue the correct frame of mind. (Ephesians 4:28, 5:3-4) It is good to be reminded that we are entitled to nothing and being deeply accustomed to certain blessings is a recipe for disaster. (Joel 2:12-14) We shouldn't underestimate Satan by testing ourselves for the vibrancy of real faith. Are you content?

Paul tells us a great mystery is wrapped up in the marriage relationship. (Eph. 5:32) Scripture speaks to every aspect of marriage with the central point being "contentment" when it comes to the marriage relationship. If you are discontent, Paul says it is because you do not have gratitude.

Give thanks in all circumstances; for this is the will of God in Christ Jesus for you. (1 Thessalonians 5:18)

When God's wants for me are brimming in the morning, as opposed to waking with an attitude of resistance (ready to complain and so forth), I know I'm starting my day with thankfulness. Thankful to have Christ. The follow-up to this is formal fellowship with Him, before setting out to obey on that given day. When my own wants are brimming in the morning, my Bible may get a cursory glance before I waste that day by gratifying my discontentment.

..but your iniquities have made a separation between you and your God, and your sins have hidden his face from you so that he does not hear. (Isaiah 59:2)

Revival implies bringing in vigor and strength - life. Restoration implies returning to and conforming to a previous standard. We are to remain in the calling in which we've been called. The meaning of "cling to" is holding onto something hard-pressed to have anyone or any circumstance remove it from one's grip. In this case, the internal motivation streamlines with the eternal for the believer who believes. Therefore, are you needing to revive your faith? Restore yourself to gladness through confession and repentance. Then pursue righteousness by obeying Him.

There is no formula for a happy marriage because you are guaranteed only one thing in this lifetime: Freedom to accept or deny the gift of salvation in Christ.

The Spirit and the Bride say, "Come." And let the one who hears say, "Come." And let the one who is thirsty come; let the one who desires take the water of life without price. (Revelation 22:17)

Heed the Word and pursue Christ with your whole heart. Apostle Paul's advice is the only advice worth repeating, thanks to and because of what Christ did for us all on the cross. Praise God.

I call heaven and earth to witness against you today, that I have set before you life and death, blessing and curse. Therefore, choose life, that you and your offspring may live, loving the Lord your God, obeying his voice and holding fast to him, for he is your life and length of days, that you may dwell in the land that the Lord swore to your fathers, to Abraham, to Isaac, and to Jacob, to give them. (Deuteronomy 30:19-20)

Chapter 18: Binding Affection

It has been four years, this month, since that awful and awesome day when my kids and I sat around the Christmas tree listening to John confess to living a fraudulent Christian life and plead for a second chance to live a rightful one with us. Our children responded favorably but not without varying degrees of broken-heartedness and anger, which needed to be expressed openly and honestly. This continues to this day.

Sin is a messy business. No one comes out of this life unscathed by the pain of being sinned against. Our only recourse is personal redemption through Jesus Christ. In time, I trust that my children will come to terms with their father's betrayal, much in the same way that John has had to come to terms with his own father's dereliction of fatherly duties and betrayal of him. All of us have to depend on Christ for all that we need to be righteous in our own lives.

For we all have sinned and fall short of the glory of God, and are justified by his grace as a gift, through redemption that is in Christ Jesus, whom God put forward as a propitiation by his blood, to be received by faith...(Romans 3:23-26)

Are you a Christian desiring a closer relationship with your spouse? Are you lonely?

John and I are in the habit of practicing hospitality and after breaking bread with many, we have become keenly aware that many Christians aren't thriving. We've also made several moves in the past few years and attended different churches, so this awareness is not limited to just one community. I think it's fair to assume that we are sensitive to the "facades" of others after what we've experienced, and based on the fact that we are willingly vulnerable with one another, we invite others to do the same and they usually end up sharing from their hearts.

From our observations, there is a lot of undue suffering due to loneliness and disenfranchisement (the state of being deprived of privileges) within our Christian communities. What privileges might some of us be deprived of as Christians? What about mutual accountability? Consider this: Had John had a brother in Christ who loved him enough to challenge him, he may have confessed to his sin sooner. Was this my husband's fault? Absolutely and absolutely not. We are called to serve and bear the burdens of one another. (Galatians 6:2)

The internet blesses us, but it also substitutes and compensates for our increasingly poor interpersonal relationships. Why exactly this is happening is debatable, but any conscientious observer can see that it constantly distracts us with its "allurements" and interferes with fellowship-driven hospitality.

By this my Father is glorified, that you bear much fruit and so prove to be my disciples. (John 15:8-9)

If not the disciples we call "brethren" and also claim to comprise our community, then with whom are we magnifying Christ? How do we adore our Lord and Master when the internet incentivizes us to seclude, withdraw, detach - ultimately be loosely connected with or outright disconnected from our church body and its other members? The ramifications for this entail a long list of "negatives" when it comes to our individual and corporate spiritual vitality.

Let love be genuine. Abhor what is evil; hold fast to what is good. Love one another with brotherly affection. Outdo one another in showing honor. Do not be slothful in zeal, be fervent in spirit, serve the Lord. (Romans 12:9-11)

My husband succeeded at keeping others from seeing the reality of his sin and brokenness. There are others like him who need other Christians to pursue them with *true zeal*—grateful servanthood. In a real sense, if I hadn't faithfully pursued John for the Lord, this brother of mine might have squandered his gift of salvation and to everyone's genuine sadness but Satan's. And what about me? Wouldn't I have wasted an opportunity to lay down my life for a friend?

Greater love has no one than this, that someone lays down his life for his friends. You are my friends if you do what I command you. (John 15:13-14)

I have written a book called *Disconnected: Why Christians Feel Lonely and Disenfranchised in this Digital Age,* and it describes why I believe many Christians suffer from loneliness and disenfranchisement and an overall unsatisfying discipleship experience. It has been described as *a scathing rebuke upon our culture.* With that in mind, my intention is to challenge all Christians. I've included a description and the Introduction in the Epilogue.

In closing, I hope my story leaves you celebrating or recognizing your need for Christ to be the center of your life. My life wasn't bad before I proclaimed Jesus Christ as my Lord and Savior thirty-three years ago, but it wasn't great either. What it lacked most was true love or the binding affection that comes with loving one's salvation in Christ more than anything else. My life outside of Christ was unsatisfying simply because we all have been created for the purpose of glorifying Him. (Isaiah 43:7)

My story, like most true stories, will not have a "Hallmark ending." I am a sinner through and through and under grace. My broken heart and wounds aren't extraordinary. There are plenty of other stories by which I can compare mine with and feel immense gratitude, with Christ's being first on that list. Next is my mother's story which includes a traumatic childhood and adolescence, two things she helped spare me of through her own personal faith. She didn't raise me perfectly, but like her, I am conditioned to look for Christ in everything and love the adventure of always finding Him. Sometimes my faith looks beautiful and orderly, but more often it feels and looks messy because that's the condition of every heart.

If you're in a difficult marriage, you know at least one area in your life where you need to practice strong faith. You are called to serve the Lord and endure any and all difficult circumstances while trusting in Him. Pray for the strength and courage to depend solely on Him for all that you need. Expect Him to answer all your prayers, if they are firmly grounded in the Word. Anticipate steadfast joy due to practicing deep and heartfelt obedience. This is the way of a Christian loyal to their first love and expecting great things.

This is the hospitality of Christ. When it comes to all suffering, one meets grace through the doorway of repentance. Once entered into His grace, the focus is on the Host, not on the guest. The focus is the hospitality of Christ and His hospitality (the act of receiving and blessing invited guests) is perfectly generous as Lord and King.

Oh, taste and see that the Lord is good! Blessed is the man who takes refuge in him! Oh fear the Lord, you his saints, for those who fear him have no lack! (Psalm 34:8-9)

The invigoration that comes with our personal trials is the Holy Spirit's charge to us to persevere in love through all the miseries of this life. The biggest misery is sin but the remedy is found in forgiveness bestowed and forgiveness received. May God bless you, and keep you, and accomplish His will for your life, starting right now, where you are at, in your time of need.

January 12, 2024 *Writing my story has accomplished an unexpected sense of profound victory. Thank you God for John. My love for him takes on a deeper meaning as I acknowledge the ultimate earthly hero in my earthly story as Jesus Christ—for it is He who has made it possible for John to reflect His love for me more than anyone else I know, and this is not a customary thing at all. . . it is a glorious thing!*

Epilogue

Shortly after John's transplant, I asked God (again) why He was withholding meaningful fellowship and hospitality from my family and me. His answer was evident in this one constant thought that held me like clay to a potter's hand. *Trust me, this will all make sense.*

The overwhelming desire of my heart was to share with others the loveliness of Christ that was revealed through my trials. After writing my first manuscript and being told that I had two conflicting themes, I separated them, and, in the end, have one book lending to my experiences and a second consisting of the lessons they imparted. Most fascinating to me has been the linear writing experience, which I greatly credit to having a close walk with God and heeding His directives placed upon my conscience.

When my angry husband said hurtful things to me, I took it to Jesus in prayer. When my friends would fellowship with me via cell phone, my need for edification came by walking and talking with Christ. When virtual strangers would try to counsel or console me over the internet, I immediately questioned why I was there seeking "fellowship" to begin with, and God answered that, too, and I stopped interacting with others in this cold and informal way. After attempting in-person reconciliation with estranged persons in my life, what I have to show for my efforts is an extensive series of texts and emails. I have cried a lot in the past few years, but I'm not ashamed. I regularly got on my knees and thanked God for loving me when others couldn't *or* wouldn't.

Christians are the only people by whom we can realistically expect to show us God's love - through their loving (Christ-inspired) words and actions. If we aren't regularly dying to self by loving others in ways that *we* know the felt love of our Lord and Savior Jesus Christ, we are failing to uphold and propagate the gospel in truth and love.

My other book addresses internet use, how and why it's hurting us, and what we should do about it. Online communication is a problem for our fellowship and community. It throws all kinds of "darts" at us, collectively and individually. Some of us use it to dodge accountability or the vulnerability of ourselves and others. Some of us capitalize on its inherent, vague way of communicating to manipulate situations involving each other. All in all, our fellowship suffers or thrives at our own hands. The great battle is won, so in a real and final sense, the internet helps and hurts our fellowship.

If you feel lonely and wonder how it is that you can feel your loneliest at church, I hope you'll read *Disconnected: Why Christians Feel Lonely and Disenfranchised in this Digital Age.*

Introduction: My Mission

If love is not flowing in our personal relationships, they grow cold by way of broken hearts, wounded egos, unresolved sin, lack of desire to reconcile, etc. A common denominator is the lack of overt acts of lovingkindness. For Christians, if their relationships fizzle with other Christians, it may be a direct result of one or both parties' abdication to uphold the gospel in truth and love, and lack of mutual affection is a symptom of this failure to love or to love well.

It can be observed during the week and perhaps you see it, too. After we part from one another's company after heartfelt singing and brief fellowship on Sunday, we return to our comforts and familiar people. With a few exceptions, we don't regularly extend hospitality to each other that day or during the week, especially to the church members we hardly know or don't know at all. We are commanded to do so. Hospitality that pleases the Lord is rooted in the gospel and stems from Christ-abiding hearts.

Now concerning brotherly love, you have no need for anyone to write to you, for you yourselves have been taught by God to love one another, for that indeed is what you are doing to all the brothers throughout Macedonia. But we urge you brothers to do this more and more (1 Thess. 4:9-10).

How does this command pertain to social media and our cell phones? American Christian hospitality is failing, and one major reason for this is we are spending vast amounts of time on our devices at the cost of esteeming one another in the faith. Since texting, social media, and the internet can't sustain our spiritual union, incessantly connecting this way is creating subtle discord and breakdown in our relationships. Without regularly demonstrating sacrificial love for one another, we exhibit disloyalty, and are at risk of breaking our covenantal vows or forgetting our duty to pursue one another for righteousness (2 Tim. 2:22).

When it comes to all of life, one meets grace through the doorway of repentance. Once we enter into His grace, our focus is on the Host, not on the guest. Our focus is the hospitality of Christ, and His hospitality (the act of receiving and blessing invited guests) is perfectly generous as Lord and King.

When it comes to Christian hospitality, we reciprocate God's gift of salvation with purpose. He meets our need for salvation through the Cross. We meet each other's material and spiritual needs by reciprocating Christ's hospitality with our own.

As a Christian whose strength is hospitality and having hosted many families and individuals over many years, my mission is clear: to use what God has revealed through my circumstances to offer a greater vision for our practice of biblical hospitality. Within this context, I hope and pray I convince you of where we are going wrong with how we use the internet and how it negatively affects our fellowship and community with one another.

"We need winds and tempests to exercise our faith, to tear off the rotten branches of self-reliance, and to root us more firmly in Christ. The day of evil reveals to us the value of our glorious hope."

- Charles Haddon Spurgeon

Made in United States
Troutdale, OR
12/20/2024

26938561R00060